MASTERING THE ART OF CONTRACT REVISION

A Practical Guide to Securing Your Commercial Agreements

Natacha Shama

CONTENTS

Title Page
Introduction — 1
Chapter 1: The Fundamentals of Commercial Contracts — 3
Chapter 2: Analyzing Contractual Clauses — 20
Chapter 3: Contract Review Methodology — 37
Chapter 4: Common Pitfalls and How to Correct Them — 50
Chapter 5: Contract Negotiation — 64
Chapter 6: Formalization and Monitoring of Contracts — 88
Conclusion — 113

INTRODUCTION

In a world where business transactions are ubiquitous, the ability to read, understand, and review a commercial contract becomes an indispensable skill. Whether you are an entrepreneur, a legal professional, a buyer, or simply someone eager to secure their transactions, knowing how to identify and correct the flaws in a contract is a valuable asset.

Commercial contracts are the backbone of business relationships. They outline the obligations of the parties, define the terms for the provision of goods and services, and provide a framework for resolving conflicts. Unfortunately, they are often drafted in complex and dense legal language, prone to pitfalls or loopholes that can have disastrous consequences.

The goal of this book is to demystify this process. You will learn not only how to read and understand commercial contracts but also how to identify and correct errors or poorly drafted clauses. Each chapter will guide you through fundamental principles, practical methodologies, and concrete examples to help you become proficient in the art of contract review.

This book is designed to be accessible to everyone. You don't need to have a legal background to follow and apply the advice it contains. Concepts are explained clearly, and the numerous examples and practical exercises will allow you to immediately put your new skills into practice.

By investing the necessary time to master the art of contract review, you gain not only legal security but also confidence during your business negotiations. You will be able to anticipate and avoid disputes, negotiate more favorable terms, and protect your interests more effectively.

Let's prepare to dive into the world of commercial contracts, discover their workings, and learn how to use them to our advantage. The journey to a better understanding of contracts begins here.

CHAPTER 1: THE FUNDAMENTALS OF COMMERCIAL CONTRACTS

1.1 Definition of a Commercial Contract

A commercial contract is a formal agreement between two or more parties who commit to fulfilling reciprocal obligations and rights in a business context. The primary objective of this type of contract is to formalize a business relationship, whether it involves the sale of goods, the provision of services, or a strategic partnership. Commercial contracts are used to secure transactions and clearly define the expectations of each party.

These contractual documents must be drafted with precision and detail to avoid any ambiguity that could lead to misunderstandings or disputes. The drafting of a commercial contract should include the following key elements:

- Contracting parties: Identification of the entities or individuals involved, their contact details, and their legal status.
- Subject of the contract: Clear and detailed description of the goods or services covered by the agreement.
- Obligations of the parties: Definition of the specific responsibilities of each party, including delivery terms, quality standards, and payment conditions.
- Contract duration: The period during which the agreement is valid, including start and end dates, as well as renewal or termination conditions.
- Financial conditions: Details regarding prices, payment terms, any additional fees, and payment deadlines.

A good commercial contract should also provide for risk management mechanisms, such as insurance, warranties, and claims management. It should also include dispute resolution clauses explaining how disputes will be handled, whether through mediation, arbitration, or legal action.

For a commercial contract to be valid, it must meet certain legal conditions. Firstly, the parties must be legally capable of contracting, meaning they must have the legal capacity to understand and agree to the terms of the agreement. Additionally, the content of the contract must be lawful and comply with current regulations.

In conclusion, a well-drafted commercial contract is an essential tool for establishing strong and lasting business relationships. It protects the interests of the parties by providing a clear and precise legal framework for their commercial interactions.

1.2 Types of Commercial Contracts

Commercial contracts come in many forms, depending on the specific needs of the parties and the nature of the transactions they govern. Understanding the different types of commercial contracts is essential to choosing the most appropriate document for each business situation. Here is an overview of the main types of commercial contracts:

Sales Contract
The sales contract is one of the most common types of commercial contracts. It governs the sale of goods between a seller and a buyer. This type of contract specifies the details of the goods sold, the agreed price, delivery conditions, as well as the obligations of each party regarding the transfer of ownership and payment.

Service Agreement
This contract formalizes the agreement between a service provider and their client. It defines the nature of the services to be provided, execution deadlines, expected quality standards, and payment conditions. This type of contract is frequently used in sectors such as consulting, technical maintenance, cleaning, and IT services.

Distribution Agreement
This type of contract governs the relationship between a product supplier and a distributor who will market these products. The distribution agreement outlines the terms of sale of the products to the distributor, the geographical distribution areas, sales targets, and the respective obligations of the parties in terms of marketing, storage, and technical support.

Franchise Agreement
The franchise agreement allows a company (the franchisor) to grant another company (the franchisee) the right to operate a brand and a know-how in exchange for royalties. This contract specifies the franchisee's obligations in terms of brand standards, initial and ongoing training, supply, and financing. It also

includes territorial and duration clauses.

Partnership Agreement

Partnership agreements formalize the collaboration between two or more parties to achieve a common goal, often by sharing resources and risks. These contracts detail the roles, financial and material contributions of each party, the distribution of profits and losses, as well as decision-making and conflict resolution mechanisms.

License Agreement

This type of contract allows one party (the licensee) to use the intellectual property of another (the licensor) in exchange for a fee. The intellectual property may include patents, trademarks, copyrights, or technical know-how. The license agreement clarifies usage rights, geographical and temporal limitations, and obligations to maintain the intellectual property in force.

Subcontracting Agreement

Subcontracting contracts are used when a company (the principal) entrusts another (the subcontractor) with the performance of certain tasks or the production of specific goods. This type of contract specifies the expected services, quality standards, delivery deadlines, and payment conditions. It often includes confidentiality and industrial property clauses.

Each type of commercial contract meets specific needs and also contains clauses tailored to the particularities of the business relationships it governs. Choosing the right type of contract is crucial to securing transactions and ensuring that all parties fulfill their contractual commitments.

1.3 The Stakeholders of a Commercial Contract

The stakeholders of a commercial contract are the entities or individuals who legally commit to respecting and executing the terms of the contract. Each stakeholder plays a crucial role in the execution of the contract and has specific rights and obligations. Understanding the role of each party is essential to ensuring that the terms of the contract are respected. Here are the main stakeholders in a commercial contract:

The Seller

The seller, or supplier, is the party that offers the goods or services within the contract. The main obligations of the seller include providing the goods or services in accordance with the contractual specifications, within the agreed timelines, and with the expected quality. The seller is also responsible for providing any relevant documentation (e.g., user manuals, warranty certificates) and adhering to the delivery conditions.

The Buyer

The buyer, or client, is the party that acquires the goods or services provided by the seller. The buyer's obligations include paying the agreed price, accepting the delivery, and adhering to the contractual conditions regarding the use of the goods or services. The buyer must also report any defects or non-conformities in the goods or services within the deadlines stipulated by the contract.

The Partner

In certain contracts, such as partnership agreements or distribution agreements, partners are stakeholders who collaborate to achieve a common goal. These partners share resources, risks, and profits. Each partner has specific roles and responsibilities defined by the contract, which may include project management, providing capital, or offering technical expertise.

The Franchisee and the Franchisor

In the context of a franchise agreement, the franchisor is the entity that grants the franchisee the right to operate its brand and know-how. The franchisor provides initial training, ongoing support, and the right to use the brand and operational systems. The franchisee is the party that operates the concept under the franchisor's brand and whose obligations include adhering to operational standards, paying royalties, and participating in ongoing training.

The Licensee and the Licensor

In a license agreement, the licensor is the party that owns the intellectual property (e.g., a patent or trademark) and grants the licensee the right to use this property. The licensor must guarantee the ownership and validity of the licensed element and may provide technical or commercial support. The licensee, in turn, is obligated to adhere to the terms of use, pay royalties, and avoid infringing on intellectual property rights beyond what is authorized by the contract.

The Subcontractor

The subcontractor is a party that performs specific tasks on behalf of the principal within the framework of a subcontracting agreement. The subcontractor's obligations include carrying out the tasks according to the agreed specifications and timelines and meeting quality standards. The principal must provide the subcontractor with all necessary elements to perform the tasks and payment for services rendered.

Third Parties

Apart from the direct parties to the contract, there may be third parties involved whose roles are specified in the contract. These may include intermediaries, guarantors, or dispute resolution entities. These third parties often play support roles to ensure the proper execution and compliance with the contractual terms.

A well-structured commercial contract should clearly identify all stakeholders and specify their roles, responsibilities, and obligations. Mutual understanding of these commitments is crucial to avoiding conflicts and ensuring smooth and efficient contract execution.

1.4 The Essential Elements of a Contract

A commercial contract must include several essential elements that ensure its validity and effectiveness. A good understanding of these elements is fundamental for drafting and reviewing strong and legally compliant contracts. Here are the main elements that a commercial contract must include:

Offer and Acceptance

A contract begins with an offer from one party and the acceptance of that offer by the other party. The offer must be clear, precise, and complete; it specifies the terms on which the offering party is willing to commit. Acceptance, on the other hand, signifies that the accepting party fully agrees to the terms of the offer, without modifications. A conditional or modified acceptance creates a counteroffer rather than a pure and simple acceptance.

Contractual Capacity

For a contract to be valid, the parties must have the legal capacity to contract. This means they must be of legal age, not subject to legal incapacity, or be duly constituted legal entities. Adults under legal protection, minors who are not emancipated, or persons under guardianship do not have the necessary legal capacity to contract, except for specific exceptions provided by law.

Legality of the Object

The contract must concern a lawful object that is not contrary to public order or morality. This means that the subject of the contract must be legally authorized. A contract concerning illegal activity or containing unlawful clauses is null and void.

Lawful Cause

The cause of the contract—the reason why the parties are entering into the contract—must also be lawful. An unlawful cause renders the contract null. A cause may be illegal if it involves illegal activities or is contrary to public interest.

General and Specific Conditions

The general conditions are standardized stipulations applicable to similar contracts, governing essential aspects such as duration, termination clauses, and liabilities. The specific conditions, however, are tailored to each individual contract and may include technical specifications, particular deadlines, or unique obligations.

Obligations of the Parties
The contract must explicitly detail the obligations of each party. This includes what each party must do to execute the contract, the deadlines by which these obligations must be fulfilled, and the conditions for delivering the services or goods. A clear description of the obligations prevents misunderstandings and facilitates the execution and monitoring of the contract.

Payment Clauses
Payment terms are a crucial element of any commercial contract. They must include the amount to be paid, payment deadlines, accepted payment methods, and penalties for late payment. These clauses protect the financial interests of the parties and ensure transparency in financial transactions.

Warranty and Liability Clauses
Warranty clauses specify the assurances provided by the seller or provider regarding the conformity and quality of the goods or services. Liability clauses define the limits of the parties' responsibility in case of defects, damages, or failure to meet contractual obligations. These clauses are essential for managing risks and providing for possible remedies.

Duration and Termination
The contract must stipulate its validity period, as well as the conditions for renewal and termination. This includes situations in which the contract may be terminated early, the notices to be given, and the consequences of termination. Specifying these elements ensures that the parties know what to expect in the event of changes in circumstances.

Dispute Resolution Clauses
It is essential to provide mechanisms for resolving potential

disputes. This may include clauses for mediation, arbitration, or recourse to competent courts. These clauses help determine how conflicts should be managed, thus minimizing uncertainties and costs associated with disputes.

Signatures of the Parties

Finally, for a contract to be valid, it must be signed by the contracting parties. The signature attests to the parties' agreement to the terms and conditions of the contract, making the agreement legally binding.

By including all these elements, a commercial contract becomes an effective tool for formalizing business relationships, protecting the parties' interests, and providing a solid basis for the implementation and execution of contractual commitments.

1.5 General Conditions and Specific Conditions

Commercial contracts consist of general conditions and specific conditions, each playing a specific role in structuring and applying the agreement. These two types of conditions help cover both standard aspects and the unique features of each contract.

General Conditions

General conditions encompass standardized clauses that apply uniformly to a category of contracts. They are designed to ensure some uniformity and cover recurring aspects in all similar contracts. Here are some common examples of clauses included in the general conditions:

- **Duration Clause:** Determines the validity period of the contract, renewal terms, and termination conditions.
- **Payment Clause:** States the payment terms, including deadlines, accepted payment methods, and penalties for delay.
- **Liability and Warranty Clause:** Defines the parties' responsibilities in case of defects or damages, as well as the warranties offered by the seller or provider.
- **Force Majeure Clause:** Anticipates exceptional circumstances that could release the parties from their obligations without penalty, such as natural disasters or armed conflicts.
- **Dispute Resolution Clause:** Indicates the methods for resolving conflicts, such as mediation, arbitration, or judicial recourse.

General conditions are often pre-drafted and minimally modified for each new contract, making them easy to use quickly and effectively.

Specific Conditions

Specific conditions, on the other hand, are tailored to each contract and adjusted based on the needs and requirements of the stakeholders. They complement the general conditions by specifying unique aspects or adapting certain standardized clauses. Here are some examples of clauses that could be included in the specific conditions:

- **Specific Objects:** Detailed description of the goods or services specific to this particular contract, including technical or performance specifications.
- **Delivery Deadlines:** Precise indication of dates and delivery methods, adapted to the client's needs and the supplier's capabilities.
- **Personalized Payment Conditions:** Adjustments to payment terms based on particular agreements between the parties, such as specific credit terms or discounts.
- **Technical or Logistical Clauses:** Provisions on specific aspects such as transport methods, storage, or installation procedures.
- **Specific Commitments of the Parties:** Additional obligations that the parties agree to respect, such as progress reports, quality audits, or specific training.

Specific conditions allow for contract customization to meet the specificities of the ongoing project or agreement, offering greater flexibility compared to the general conditions.

Integration of General and Specific Conditions

When drafting a contract, it is crucial to harmoniously integrate the general and specific conditions. A common approach is to include the general conditions first as the contract's foundation, followed by a separate section for the specific conditions. This structure allows the parties to clearly understand which clauses apply in a standardized manner and which are specifically adapted to their agreement.

It is also important to ensure consistency between the general and specific conditions. The general conditions should not contradict the specific conditions, and all differences should be clarified to avoid any ambiguity or conflict of interpretation. In case of a contradiction, the contract should specify which section prevails, usually favoring the specific conditions.

In conclusion, the general and specific conditions form the backbone of commercial contracts, combining stability and flexibility. A clear understanding and careful drafting of these conditions are essential to ensuring the legal validity of the contract and the satisfaction of the stakeholders.

1.6 The Legality and Validity of Contracts

For a commercial contract to be legally binding and enforceable, it must meet several conditions of legality and validity. Ensuring the legality and validity of contracts is crucial for any business relationship, as a non-compliant contract can be contested and annulled by a court. Here are the main aspects to consider to ensure that a contract is legal and valid:

Legal Capacity of the Parties

For a contract to be valid, the contracting parties must have the legal capacity to engage their responsibility. This means they must be of legal age, mentally competent, and free from any legal restrictions concerning their capacity to contract. For legal entities such as companies, this implies that the signatory representatives are duly authorized to act on behalf of the company.

Free and Informed Consent

The consent of the parties must be free and informed. A contract signed under duress, threat, or undue influence can be annulled. Similarly, the parties must be fully informed and understand the terms of the contract. Any form of fraud, deceit, or significant error can also lead to the annulment of the contract.

Legality of the Object

The object of the contract must be lawful. A contract concerning illegal activity, contrary to public order, or morality is null and void. This means that the obligations stipulated in the contract must comply with the laws and regulations in force at the time of its conclusion.

Lawful Cause

The cause of the contract, i.e., the reason why the parties are contracting, must also be lawful. An unlawful or immoral cause can result in the nullity of the contract. The cause must be explicit and aligned with legal and ethical principles.

Formal Compliance
Some categories of contracts must comply with specific formalities to be valid. For example, some contracts must be in writing, while others require registration or the presence of witnesses. The omission of these formalities can affect the validity of the contract.

Determination of Performances
The performances that are the subject of the contract must be determined or determinable. This means that the rights and obligations of each party must be clearly defined and understandable. A vague or ambiguous contract may be deemed unenforceable. The performances must be sufficiently precise so that each party knows exactly what is expected of them.

Absence of Defects in Consent
For a contract to be valid, it must not be tainted by defects in consent. These defects include error, fraud (intentional deception), duress (physical or moral coercion), and lesion (manifest imbalance in performances). The presence of one of these defects may lead to the annulment of the contract.

Consistency and Integrity of the Contract
A contract must be consistent and complete. Any significant inconsistency or omission can cause interpretation issues and lead to disputes. Appendices, addendums, and supplementary documents must be clearly referenced and integrated into the main contract to ensure its integrity.

Registration and Conservation
Depending on the nature of the contract and the competent jurisdiction, it may be necessary to register it with an administrative or judicial authority. This ensures proof of the contract's existence and can facilitate its enforcement. Additionally, contracts must be stored securely to be produced in case of a dispute.

Consequences of Invalidity
An invalid contract has no binding force and cannot produce legal effects. The parties cannot demand the execution of an invalid

contract, and each party may request the return of performances made. Furthermore, in the case of invalidity due to illegality, criminal sanctions may be considered depending on the context.

In conclusion, the legality and validity of a contract depend on meeting several essential conditions. Particular attention must be paid to these aspects when drafting and reviewing commercial contracts to protect the parties' interests and ensure the legal security of their transactions.

CHAPTER 2: ANALYZING CONTRACTUAL CLAUSES

Now that we have explored the fundamentals of commercial contracts, it is crucial to focus on the elements that compose these essential documents. Each clause in a commercial contract carries importance and can significantly influence the terms of the agreement. In the next chapter, we will examine in detail the various contractual clauses, identifying the most common ones and learning how to spot those that could pose problems.

2.1 Common Clauses in Commercial Contracts

Commercial contracts often include a set of common clauses designed to standardize and regulate the key aspects of the contractual relationship. Although each contract may have its peculiarities, certain clauses frequently appear due to their legal and practical importance. Here is an overview of the common clauses typically found in commercial contracts:

Confidentiality Clause

The confidentiality clause requires the parties not to disclose certain information obtained during their collaboration. This can include trade secrets, financial data, market strategies, or any information designated as confidential. This clause aims to protect the commercial interests of the parties and maintain the confidentiality of sensitive information.

Non-Compete Clause

This clause prevents the parties from engaging in competitive activities during the contract's duration, and often for a specified period after its termination. It aims to protect the interests of one party by preventing the other from using information obtained during the contractual relationship for competitive purposes.

Liability Clause

The liability clause determines the responsibilities of the parties in case of a breach of contractual obligations. It may include limitations or exclusions of liability for certain types of damages, such as indirect losses or intangible damages. This clause is crucial for managing and anticipating the financial risks associated with the contract's execution.

Force Majeure Clause

The force majeure clause provides for exceptional circumstances that could prevent the fulfillment of contractual obligations, such as natural disasters, conflicts, strikes, or other unforeseen events. This clause often specifies the conditions under which a party may be exempted from its obligations without penalty due to these events.

Penalties Clause
This clause imposes financial penalties in case of non-compliance with contractual obligations, such as delivery delays or failure to meet quality standards. Penalties can be fixed or calculated based on the duration or severity of the breach. They encourage the parties to meet their commitments by adding a financial dimension to the obligations.

Termination Clause
The termination clause outlines the conditions under which the contract can be ended before its natural expiration. It may provide for specific grounds for termination, such as a severe breach of a contractual obligation, the bankruptcy of a party, or legislative changes affecting the agreement. The clause also specifies the formalities to be observed, such as notice periods and possible compensations.

Renewal Clause
The renewal clause stipulates the conditions for extending the contract upon the expiration of its initial term. It may provide for automatic renewal under certain conditions or require written agreement from the parties. This clause is important for ensuring the continuity of business relationships without interruption.

Intellectual Property Clause
This clause determines the ownership and use of intellectual property rights created or used within the framework of the contract. It often specifies to which party the inventions, creations, patents, trademarks, and other intellectual assets belong. It may also include licenses granted to the other party for usage.

Price Revision Clause
The price revision clause allows for the adjustment of prices for goods or services based on market fluctuations, changes in production costs, or other economic criteria. It generally provides a calculation mechanism and conditions under which prices can

be revised, protecting the parties against unforeseen variations.

Dispute Resolution Clause

The dispute resolution clause specifies the mechanisms provided for resolving potential conflicts between the parties. It may include procedures for mediation, arbitration, or recourse to the courts. This clause is essential for defining a clear and predefined framework for resolving disputes, thus reducing uncertainties and costs associated with litigation.

By grouping these common clauses, commercial contracts can offer a coherent and comprehensive legal framework to govern business relationships. Each clause plays a specific role and contributes to achieving the contractual objectives by protecting the interests and defining the responsibilities of the involved parties.

2.2 Identifying Abusive Clauses

Abusive clauses in commercial contracts are stipulations that create a significant imbalance between the rights and obligations of the parties, to the detriment of the weaker party. These clauses are often perceived as unfair and may be invalidated by the courts. Identifying and eliminating abusive clauses is essential to ensure contractual fairness and the legal validity of a contract. Here's how to recognize common abusive clauses:

Excessively Limiting Liability Clauses

Clauses that disproportionately limit one party's liability to the point of making it almost inapplicable can be considered abusive. For example, a clause that excludes all liability of the supplier for product defects, including serious damage caused to property or persons.

Unilateral Termination Clauses

A clause that allows only one party to terminate the contract at any time, without notice or justification, while the other party is subject to strict constraints for termination, is abusive. This creates an imbalance where one party has disproportionate control over the continuity of the contract.

Clauses Imposing Excessive Penalties

Clauses that impose excessive financial penalties for breaches or delays in fulfilling obligations can be deemed abusive. For instance, a very high penalty for a minor payment delay relative to the overall value of the contract.

Unilateral Modification Clauses

Clauses that allow one party to unilaterally modify essential terms of the contract, such as prices, services provided, or delivery deadlines, without the other party's consent, are often considered abusive. They deprive the other party of any control or recourse in the face of unforeseen changes.

Clauses Limiting Rights of Recourse

A clause that restricts a party's right to seek remedy in case of a dispute, by limiting access to the courts or imposing strict conditions for taking legal action, can be abusive. This includes forced arbitration clauses with conditions that are disadvantageous only to one party.

Disadvantageous Automatic Renewal Clauses
Automatic renewal clauses that force a party to continue the contract under unfavorable conditions, without an easy way to terminate before renewal, can be abusive. This is especially true if the notice period for termination is excessively long or complicated compared to the contract's duration.

Clauses Imposing Disproportionate Obligations
Clauses that impose very heavy or costly obligations on one party while only requiring light obligations or significant benefits for the other party can be identified as abusive. An example would be a clause requiring a minor partner to make substantial investments without any guarantee of return.

Excessive Guarantee Clauses
Clauses that demand excessive and unreasonable guarantees from only one party, such as disproportionate securities or costly insurance, can also be abusive. These requirements should be proportionate and justified by the contract's risks.

Unbalanced Confidentiality Clauses
Confidentiality clauses that impose strict restrictions on only one party while allowing the other party to freely exploit or disclose confidential information create an obvious imbalance. A good contract should include reciprocal and fair confidentiality obligations.

Restrictive Exclusivity Clauses
Exclusivity clauses that prevent a party from collaborating or doing business with other partners or suppliers for an extended period or under strict conditions can be deemed abusive, especially if they seriously limit growth or diversification opportunities.

How to Avoid and Correct Abusive Clauses
To avoid and correct abusive clauses, it is crucial to draft balanced contracts negotiated in good faith. Here are some steps:

- **Legal Review:** Have the contract reviewed by a legal advisor to identify and correct potentially abusive clauses.
- **Fair Negotiation:** Ensure a transparent negotiation process where the concerns and requirements of both parties are heard and respected.
- **Fair Recourse Clauses:** Include recourse clauses that offer fair solutions in case of disputes, such as neutral mediation or arbitration.
- **Verification of Obligations:** Compare the obligations imposed on each party to ensure they are proportional and fair.
- **Mutual Consensus:** Obtain the informed consent of both parties for all clauses, ensuring that neither party feels coerced or disadvantaged.

By identifying and correcting abusive clauses, the parties can establish contracts that promote sustainable and fair business relationships while protecting their respective interests. Balanced and fair contracts are more likely to withstand the test of time and prevent disputes.

2.3 Specific Clauses for Certain Types of Contracts

Commercial contracts can vary significantly depending on the type of transaction or the nature of the relationship between the parties. As a result, some contracts require specific clauses tailored to their particular context. Here is an overview of specific clauses for certain common types of commercial contracts:

Sales Contract

- **Product Compliance Clause:** Specifies the quality and performance standards that the products must meet, as well as the quality control procedures.
- **Retention of Title Clause:** Stipulates that ownership of the sold goods remains with the seller until full payment of the price by the buyer.
- **Delivery and Risk Transfer Clause:** Details the delivery terms, the incoterms (e.g., FOB, CIF) used to determine the point of transfer of the risk of loss or damage to the goods.

Service Agreement

- **Service Level Agreement (SLA) Clause:** Defines the performance and service levels (response time, availability, maintenance) that the service provider commits to meet.
- **Service Evaluation Clause:** Specifies the methods for evaluating and reporting service quality, including periodic evaluations and performance audits.
- **Training and Support Clause:** Details the service provider's obligations in terms of providing training and technical support to the buyer or its users.

Distribution Agreement

- **Exclusive Territory Clause:** Grants the distributor the exclusive right to sell the supplier's products in a specific geographic area.

- **Sales Objectives Clause:** Establishes the sales targets to be met by the distributor and the consequences of failing to meet these targets.
- **Product Return Clause:** Specifies the conditions and procedures for returning unsold or defective products to the supplier.

Franchise Agreement

- **Operational Manuals Clause:** Requires the franchisee to comply with the operational manuals provided by the franchisor.
- **Royalties and Fees Clause:** Details the amounts the franchisee must pay to the franchisor, often in the form of fixed fees or a percentage of turnover.
- **Advertising and Marketing Clause:** Specifies the franchisee's obligations regarding participation in advertising and marketing campaigns centralized by the franchisor.

Partnership Agreement

- **Profit and Loss Sharing Clause:** Establishes the terms for distributing the profits generated and the losses incurred within the partnership.
- **Capital and Skills Contribution Clause:** Details the financial and in-kind contributions that each partner must provide to achieve the partnership's goals.
- **Governance Clause:** Specifies the terms of managing the partnership, including strategic decision-making and conflict resolution between partners.

License Agreement

- **Scope of License Clause:** Defines the geographical, temporal, and domain limits for the use of the intellectual property rights granted.
- **Royalty Clause:** Details the calculation and payment

terms for royalties due by the licensee to the licensor.
- **Intellectual Property Validity Guarantee Clause:** Commits the licensor to ensure that the intellectual property remains valid and enforceable throughout the contract's duration.

Subcontracting Agreement
- **Compliance with Specifications Clause:** Requires the subcontractor to adhere to the technical and quality specifications defined by the principal.
- **Monitoring and Audit Clause:** Grants the principal the right to monitor and audit the subcontractor's activities to verify compliance and quality of the work performed.
- **Indemnification Clause:** Specifies the obligations for compensation in case of non-compliance with contractual conditions by the subcontractor, including financial penalties and compensation for damages incurred.

Adapting and Including Specific Clauses

When drafting or reviewing commercial contracts, it is essential to identify the relevant specific clauses for the type of contract in question. Including these clauses ensures that all particular aspects of the contract are covered, thus reducing the risks of disputes and misunderstandings. Furthermore, these specific clauses should be drafted clearly and in detail to ensure their correct interpretation and execution in line with the parties' expectations.

By integrating specific clauses tailored to the type of contract, the parties can better protect their interests and structure their business relationships in a fair and balanced manner, contributing to sustainable and effective partnerships.

2.4 Techniques for Analyzing Clauses

Analyzing the clauses of a commercial contract is a methodical process that allows for verifying the conformity, clarity, and fairness of the agreed terms. Although it may seem complex, a few proven techniques make this analysis easier. Here is a structured approach to effectively evaluating the clauses of a commercial contract:

Active and Thorough Reading

The first step is an active and thorough reading of the contract. This involves carefully reading each clause, noting any technical or legal terms that are not understood for further research. A thorough reading ensures that each clause is examined and that nothing is overlooked.

Internal Consistency Check

It is crucial to check that all the clauses in the contract are consistent with each other. Clauses should not contradict each other or create ambiguities. For example, delivery deadlines mentioned in one clause should match the payment deadlines indicated elsewhere in the contract.

Identifying Key Clauses

Identifying the key clauses of the contract is an important step. This includes clauses on payment, delivery, liability, termination, and any other clauses that are critical to the contract's execution. Particular attention should be paid to these clauses to ensure that they are clear, fair, and balanced.

Legal Terms Analysis

The specific legal terms used in the contract must be well understood. It may be useful to consult legal resources or seek advice from a legal advisor to clarify technical terms. A good understanding of these terms is essential to avoid misinterpretations.

Legality and Compliance Verification

Clauses should be scrutinized to verify their legality and

compliance with applicable regulations. This includes ensuring that the clauses respect the parties' rights, local and international laws, and industry standards. An illegal or non-compliant clause could invalidate all or part of the contract.

Balance Evaluation of Clauses

Each clause should be evaluated to ensure it is balanced and does not disproportionately favor one party. Abusive or unbalanced clauses, such as those imposing excessive penalties or strict unilateral obligations, should be adjusted to ensure a fair relationship between the parties.

Clarity and Precision Check

Clauses should be drafted in a clear and precise manner to avoid any ambiguity. Vague or open-to-interpretation formulations should be avoided. Every obligation and right should be clearly defined to ensure mutual understanding of the contractual terms.

Comparison with Models and Standards

Comparing the contract's clauses with standard models and industry norms can help identify omissions or irregularities. This comparison can also provide ideas for additions or modifications to improve the contract's structure and content.

Use of Checklists

Using specific checklists for contract analysis can be very helpful. These lists ensure that all necessary clauses are present and correct. They serve as a guide to systematically reviewing each important aspect of the contract.

Simulation and Scenario Testing

Simulating possible situations and testing how the contract's clauses respond to these scenarios is a practical technique for evaluating their effectiveness. For example, in case of a delivery delay, check the contract's recourse mechanisms and the penalties provided.

Consulting a Legal Expert

Finally, seeking advice from a legal expert, especially for complex or large-scale contracts, is often indispensable. A lawyer or legal advisor can provide in-depth analysis and identify potential issues that may escape a non-specialist.

Tools and Resources for Analysis

- **Contract Management Software:** These tools can help identify key clauses, verify compliance, and analyze the risks associated with the contractual terms.
- **Legal Guides and Manuals:** Consulting legal guides can provide detailed explanations of commonly used terms and conditions.
- **Legal Databases:** Access to legal databases containing case law and contract models can be valuable for a better understanding of accepted norms and practices.

By employing these analysis techniques, parties can ensure that the contract clauses are fair, clear, compliant, and effective, thereby strengthening the stability and durability of their business relationships.

2.5 Case Study: Analysis of a Sample Contract

To illustrate the techniques and concepts discussed in the previous sections, we will conduct a case study by analyzing a sample contract. This practical exercise will allow us to apply the methods of clause analysis and identify any weaknesses or imbalances that may exist. Here is an example of a service agreement:

Contract Context

- **Contracting Parties:**
    - **Service Provider:** XYZ Services SARL
    - **Client:** ABC Entreprise SA
- **Contract Subject:** IT maintenance services for a duration of 12 months.
- **Total Contract Amount:** 50,000 EUR, payable monthly.

Contract Content

1. **Contract Subject**
    - XYZ Services SARL undertakes to provide IT maintenance services to ABC Entreprise SA's facilities, covering repair, maintenance, and technical support for a period of 12 months.

2. **Duration and Termination**
    - The contract takes effect from January 1, 2023, for a duration of 12 months.
    - Each party may terminate the contract with 60 days' notice in the event of a serious breach of contractual obligations.

3. **Confidentiality Obligation**
    - Both parties agree to keep confidential all information exchanged under this contract during the contract period and for a period of 2

years after its termination.

4. **Payment Terms**
   - The total contract amount is 50,000 EUR, payable in 12 monthly installments of 4,166.67 EUR each, to be paid before the 5th of each month.
   - In case of late payment, a penalty of 1% of the due amount will be applied for each month of delay.

5. **Non-Compete Clause**
   - XYZ Services SARL agrees not to provide similar services to a competitor of ABC Entreprise SA during the contract period and for 6 months after its termination.

6. **Warranty and Liability**
   - XYZ Services SARL guarantees the quality of the services provided and undertakes to repair any failure reported by ABC Entreprise SA within 48 hours.
   - The liability of XYZ Services SARL is limited to the total contract amount in case of direct damages caused by its services.

7. **Force Majeure**
   - Neither party will be held responsible for a delay or failure in performing its contractual obligations caused by a force majeure event, as defined by the Civil Code.

8. **Disputes and Jurisdiction**
   - In case of a dispute arising from this contract, the parties agree to attempt to resolve it amicably before resorting to the courts.
   - Failing an amicable resolution, the dispute will be submitted to the jurisdiction of the courts of

[Designated Location].

Analysis of the Sample Contract

Contract Subject

- **Clarity:** The contract subject is clearly defined, indicating the specific services provided.
- **Completeness:** The maintenance services are well described, but it would be useful to further detail the types of maintenance covered (preventive, corrective).

Duration and Termination

- **Consistency:** The clause is consistent with standard practices, offering reasonable notice for termination.
- **Balance:** The conditions for termination due to a serious breach are fair, but it might be useful to add termination for convenience with equitable compensation.

Confidentiality Obligation

- **Clarity:** This clause is well-formulated and precise.
- **Completeness:** The post-contract period of 2 years for confidentiality is reasonable and reflects a concern for protecting sensitive information.

Payment Terms

- **Clarity and Precision:** The payment terms and late payment penalties are clearly defined, helping to avoid disputes related to payment.
- **Balance:** A penalty of 1% per month is reasonable and in line with industry standards.

Non-Compete Clause

- **Clarity:** The duration and scope of non-competition are specified.
- **Balance:** The 6-month period after termination is reasonable, but the clause could be drafted to avoid an overly broad definition of "competitor."

Warranty and Liability

- **Limitation:** The limitation of liability to the total contract amount is a common practice but should be verified for acceptability by ABC Entreprise SA.
- **Balance:** The 48-hour repair warranty is favorable to the buyer.

Force Majeure

- **Clarity:** The definition of force majeure is standard and compliant with civil law.
- **Completeness:** This clause is adequate and protects both parties in case of unforeseen events.

Disputes and Jurisdiction

- **Clarity:** The dispute clause initially favors an amicable resolution, which is positive.
- **Completeness:** Directly indicating the designated courts as the competent jurisdiction ensures that the parties know where to act legally.

Conclusion

This case study demonstrates the importance of analyzing each clause of a contract to ensure its clarity, balance, and legal compliance. By applying the clause analysis techniques discussed earlier, we can identify the strengths and weaknesses of the sample contract and propose adjustments to enhance the protection of the parties and the legal robustness of the agreement.

CHAPTER 3: CONTRACT REVIEW METHODOLOGY

After understanding the various clauses that make up a commercial contract, it's time to focus on the methods for reviewing these documents. A thorough review can prevent many disputes and ensure that all parties adhere to their obligations. In this chapter, we will detail the steps and techniques for conducting an effective and comprehensive contract review.

3.1 Preparation for Review

To undertake an effective review of a commercial contract, careful preparation is essential. This preliminary step ensures that you approach the review with a clear understanding and optimal organization. Here are the key aspects to consider when preparing for a contract review:

Understanding the Context

Before beginning the review, it is vital to understand the context in which the contract was drafted. This includes:

- **The Contracting Parties:** Clearly identify the parties involved, their roles, and their respective objectives.
- **The Purpose of the Contract:** Understand the primary goal of the contract and the services or products it covers.
- **The Legal and Regulatory Environment:** Familiarize yourself with the laws and regulations applicable to this type of contract and the relevant jurisdiction.

Gathering Necessary Documents

Collect all relevant documents necessary for the review, including:

- **Previous Versions of the Contract:** Compare different versions to identify changes and developments.
- **Reference Documents:** Include standards, regulatory guidelines, and similar case studies for a comparative evaluation.
- **Correspondence and Negotiations:** All exchanges between the parties can provide useful information about the intentions and unwritten agreements.

Organizing the Workspace

Create an environment conducive to the review by:

- **Designating a Quiet Space:** Work in an area where you can concentrate without interruptions.
- **Using Review Tools:** Equip yourself with document

management software, collaborative editing tools, and version comparison tools.

Planning the Review Process

Develop a detailed plan to approach the contract review:

- **Define Objectives:** Specify what needs to be checked, modified, or clarified in the contract.
- **Allocate Necessary Time:** Prepare a realistic schedule that includes deadlines for each important section or clause.
- **Involve Stakeholders:** Identify key individuals within each contracting party whose input is necessary and plan meetings or checkpoints.

Legal Training

Ensure that all individuals involved in the review possess adequate training:

- **Training Sessions:** Organize legal training sessions for the teams involved so they understand legal and contractual principles.
- **Access to Legal Advisors:** Ensure easy access to legal experts to address specific questions that may arise.

Use of Checklists

Prepare one or more checklists to guide you through the review:

- **Essential Clauses Checklist:** List the essential clauses that every contract should contain.
- **Legal Checkpoints Checklist:** Include all legal aspects to verify, such as regulatory compliance and arbitration clauses.

Review Software and Tools

Leverage digital tools to facilitate and accelerate your work:

- **Text Comparison Software:** Use tools that allow you to compare different versions of the contract to detect changes.
- **Collaborative Editing Tools:** Adopt platforms where

multiple users can work simultaneously on the same document.

Psychological Preparation

Contract review can be intellectually demanding:

- **Maintain Focus:** Prepare to work in review sessions, interspersed with regular breaks to avoid mental fatigue.
- **Stress Management:** Adopt stress management techniques to stay calm and effective.

By following these preparation steps, you will be better equipped to approach the contract review systematically and thoroughly. Good preparation minimizes errors, clarifies ambiguities, and ensures that the revised contract will be solid, balanced, and legally compliant.

3.2 Careful Reading and Clause-by-Clause Analysis

Careful reading and clause-by-clause analysis form the core of contract review. This step requires special attention to identify any errors, ambiguities, or imbalances that may exist in the contract. Here's how to proceed systematically:

Methodology for Careful Reading

Initial Global Reading

- **Objective:** Gain an overview of the contract.
- **Action:** Read the document from start to finish without making any modifications, taking notes on points that require further examination.

Second Detailed Reading

- **Objective:** Begin in-depth analysis of each clause.
- **Action:** Read each clause slowly and methodically, ensuring that you fully understand every term and condition.

Clause-by-Clause Analysis

Identifying Key Clauses

- **Duration and Termination Clause:** Verify that the contract duration and termination conditions are clearly defined and fair to both parties.
- **Payment Clause:** Ensure that the payment terms are detailed, including deadlines, payment methods, and penalties for late payment.
- **Liability Clause:** Examine liability limitations to ensure they are reasonable and industry-standard.
- **Confidentiality Clause:** Check that confidentiality obligations are balanced and clearly specified.

Validating Clarity and Precision

- **Clarity of Language:** Avoid vague or ambiguous terms.

Each condition should be explicitly and predictably formulated.

- **Precision of Obligations:** Each party's obligations must be described precisely and unequivocally.

Verifying Legal Compliance

- **Regulatory Compliance:** Verify that the clauses comply with applicable laws and regulations in the relevant jurisdiction.
- **Validity of Clauses:** Some clauses may be invalid or unenforceable, such as disproportionate penalty clauses or unfair clauses.

Evaluating the Balance of Clauses

- **Fairness:** Ensure that the clauses do not unduly favor one party. Obligations and rights should be balanced.
- **Abusive Clauses:** Identify and modify clauses that could be considered abusive by a court.

Checking the Details

- **Meticulousness:** Details such as amounts, dates, and figures must be accurate and consistent.
- **Cross-References:** Ensure that all internal references (e.g., "see section 3.2") are correct.

Information Security

- **Data Protection:** Ensure that confidentiality and personal data protection clauses comply with regulations such as GDPR.

Use of Review Tools

Contract Review Software

- **Text Comparison:** Use software that allows you to compare different versions of the contract to identify changes.
- **Annotations and Comments:** Insert annotations and comments to document your observations and suggestions for modification.

Checklists and Dashboards
- **Review Checklist:** Use a checklist to ensure that all important clauses are present and correct.
- **Dashboard:** Create a dashboard to track sections and clauses that require modification, additions, or clarifications.

Collaboration and Validation

Involving Experts
- **Legal Review:** Seek the opinion of legal advisors to validate the compliance and robustness of clauses.
- **Stakeholder Consultation:** Involve key stakeholders to obtain their feedback and approvals on proposed changes.

Finalizing the Analysis
- **Synthesis of Modifications:** Document all proposed changes and the reasons for these changes.
- **Final Validation:** Review the final version of the contract with all stakeholders to obtain consensus before finalizing.

By conducting a careful reading and detailed analysis of each clause, you can ensure that the revised contract is clear, precise, balanced, and compliant with legal requirements. This analytical rigor greatly contributes to the solidity and durability of the contractual agreement.

3.3 Checklist of Points to Verify

Reviewing a commercial contract requires meticulous attention to detail. To help structure this process, a checklist of points to verify can be extremely useful. Here is a comprehensive checklist covering the main aspects to consider when reviewing your contract:

Identity of the Parties

- **Full Names and Contact Details:** Verify that the names, addresses, and contact information of each party are correct and complete.
- **Legal Status:** Ensure that the legal status of each party (company, individual, association) is clearly indicated.

Contract Context

- **Purpose of the Contract:** Confirm that the purpose of the contract is clearly defined and described.
- **Duration and Dates:** Check the start and end dates, as well as any stipulations regarding the contract's duration.

Financial Terms

- **Payment Terms:** Ensure that the payment terms (amount, deadlines, methods) are clearly stated.
- **Billing Conditions:** Verify billing deadlines, reimbursement conditions, and terms in case of late payment.

Obligations of the Parties

- **Description of Services or Products:** The services or products provided must be described in detail and precisely.
- **Performance Standards and Criteria:** Specify the performance or quality standards that the services or products must meet.
- **Execution Deadlines:** Check that execution or delivery

deadlines are specifically indicated.

Liability Clauses

- **Limitation of Liability:** Ensure that any limitation of liability is clearly defined and reasonable.
- **Indemnification Obligations:** Verify indemnification clauses to ensure they are fair and appropriate.

Confidentiality and Intellectual Property

- **Confidentiality Clause:** Confirm that confidentiality obligations are balanced and specific to sensitive information.
- **Intellectual Property:** Verify provisions related to intellectual property, including licenses and usage rights.

Force Majeure Clauses

- **Definition and Conditions:** Ensure that the force majeure clause is well-defined and covers relevant unforeseen events.
- **Consequences on Obligations:** Check how the parties' obligations are affected by force majeure events.

Modification and Amendment Clauses

- **Modification Procedure:** Ensure that the procedure for amending the contract is clearly described.
- **Mutual Consent:** Verify that any modification requires the written consent of all parties.

Termination Clauses

- **Termination Conditions:** Confirm the specific conditions under which the contract can be terminated by either party.
- **Termination Notice:** Check the notice periods required for proper termination.

Dispute Resolution Clauses

- **Resolution Mechanisms:** Ensure that dispute resolution mechanisms (mediation, arbitration, competent courts) are specified.

- **Jurisdiction:** Verify that the jurisdiction in case of dispute is clearly specified.

Regulatory Requirements and Compliance

- **Compliance with Applicable Laws:** Verify that the contract mentions compliance with applicable laws and regulations.
- **Mandatory Clauses:** Ensure that all legally mandatory clauses are included.

Contract Execution

- **Signatures:** Verify that the contract provides for the parties' signatures, including electronic signature provisions if applicable.
- **Summary of Attached Documents:** Confirm that all attached or referenced documents in the contract are listed and attached.

Final Check

- **Internal Consistency:** Ensure that all clauses are consistent with each other and do not contradict.
- **Spelling and Grammar:** Check that there are no spelling or grammar errors in the final document.
- **Double-Checking:** Perform a second review or ask another expert to review the contract to identify potential errors.

By following this rigorous checklist, you can ensure that all key aspects of the contract have been examined and validated, reducing the risk of disputes and misunderstandings between the parties. A methodical and detailed approach will guarantee the robustness and fairness of your commercial contract.

3.4 Tools and Techniques for an Effective Review

Reviewing a commercial contract with precision and efficiency requires the use of specialized tools and proven techniques. The goal is to ensure that the contract is clear, balanced, and legally compliant. Here is a selection of tools and techniques that can greatly facilitate this process:

Digital Tools

Contract Management Software

- **Features:** Allow storage, organization, and management of contracts in one place. They offer advanced search capabilities, deadline reminders, and change tracking.
- **Examples:** DocuSign, ContractWorks, PandaDoc.

Text Comparison Applications

- **Features:** Facilitate the comparison of different versions of a contract by highlighting changes made. They help quickly identify changes between two documents.
- **Examples:** WinMerge, Draftable, Workshare Compare.

Collaborative Editing Tools

- **Features:** Allow multiple users to work simultaneously on the same document, add comments, and track changes in real time.
- **Examples:** Google Docs, Microsoft Word Online, Slack (for communication).

Legal Databases

- **Features:** Provide access to a large collection of case law, contract templates, and relevant laws. They help verify the legal compliance of clauses.
- **Examples:** LexisNexis, Westlaw, Dalloz.

Review Techniques

Structural Analysis

- **Description:** Break the contract into logical sections and subsections to facilitate the review. This ensures that the contract follows a coherent order and includes all important clauses.
- **Method:** Use clear headers and subheadings for each section, write a descriptive summary.

Repeated Reading

- **Description:** Read the contract multiple times, both globally to understand the whole and in detail to delve into each clause.
- **Method:** Alternate between slow readings for in-depth understanding and fast readings to identify inconsistencies.

Use of Checklists

- **Description:** Use checklists to ensure that all essential elements are present and correct in the contract.
- **Method:** Compare each part of the contract with your checklist to identify omissions or errors.

Scenario Simulation

- **Description:** Test the contract by simulating possible scenarios that could arise during its execution. This helps assess the robustness of the clauses.
- **Method:** Create fictional case studies or base them on previous situations to test the responsiveness of clauses.

Consultation with Experts

- **Description:** Call on legal advisors or industry experts to get professional opinions on complex or ambiguous clauses.
- **Method:** Organize review sessions with experts to discuss sensitive points and obtain approvals.

Annotations and Comments

- **Description:** Annotate the contract with comments to clarify important points or note questions and

suggestions.
- **Method:** Use annotation features in digital documents or margins for printed documents.

Cross-Review Groups
- **Description:** Form groups within your organization for cross-reviewing documents. This helps benefit from diverse insights and spot errors that one might miss themselves.
- **Method:** Organize peer review sessions and discuss points raised in evaluation meetings.

Advanced Techniques

Continuous Training
- **Description:** Regularly train your team on the latest practices and regulatory changes to stay up-to-date on best practices in contract review.
- **Method:** Attend seminars, online courses, and specialized workshops.

By integrating these tools and techniques into your review process, you can ensure a thorough and rigorous analysis of commercial contracts. This not only helps detect errors or omissions but also improves the clarity, legal validity, and balance of contractual agreements.

CHAPTER 4: COMMON PITFALLS AND HOW TO CORRECT THEM

With a clear methodology for contract review, we must now focus on recognizing and correcting common pitfalls. Even the best-drafted contracts can contain errors or ambiguities. In this chapter, we will identify frequent mistakes in commercial contracts and propose strategies to correct them effectively.

4.1 Frequent Errors in Commercial Contracts

Despite the best intentions, errors often find their way into commercial contracts. Identifying these common errors helps in avoiding them and drafting stronger, more balanced contracts. Here are some of the frequently encountered errors in commercial contracts:

Ambiguities and Vague Language

Using vague or ambiguous terms can lead to differing interpretations and disputes. For example, phrases like "as soon as possible" or "reasonably acceptable" lack precision. Clear and precise language is crucial to avoid misunderstandings.

Important Omissions

Forgetting essential clauses can compromise the validity and enforceability of the contract. For instance, not including a force majeure or termination clause can leave parties without adequate recourse in unforeseen situations.

Incomplete Definitions

Failing to clearly define specific terms related to the agreement can lead to disagreements. Each technical term or jargon used should be clearly defined in a dedicated definitions section.

Duplicate or Contradictory Clauses

Including duplicate or contradictory clauses can create confusion and weaken the contract. Each section should be unique, and all clauses should be consistent with one another.

Non-Compliant Legal Provisions

Incorporating clauses that do not comply with current laws and regulations can render the contract partially or completely void. It is essential to ensure that each clause meets relevant legal requirements.

Poor Management of Dates and Deadlines

Mismanaging or incorrectly indicating dates and deadlines—such as payment due dates, delivery dates, and termination periods—can create compliance and execution problems. Each deadline must be clearly stipulated and realistic.

Unreasonable Limitation of Liability

Excessively limiting one party's liability can be perceived as abusive and may not hold up in court. Limitations must be reasonable and equitable to be accepted by all parties.

Omission of Termination Conditions

Failing to include specific termination conditions can lead to difficulties when parties wish to end the agreement. Termination grounds and necessary notices should be clearly defined.

Inadequate Warranty Clauses

Vague or insufficient warranty clauses can leave parties without adequate protection in case of failure. Warranties must be explicitly defined, including conditions, duration, and remedies.

Confidentiality Issues

Ignoring confidentiality needs or having incomplete confidentiality clauses can expose parties to data breaches. A comprehensive and strictly defined confidentiality clause is essential to protect sensitive information.

Examples of Frequent Errors

- **Incorrect Party Names:** Misspelling a party's name or using a trade name instead of the full legal name.
- **Lack of Signatures:** Leaving a contract unsigned by the required parties makes the agreement unenforceable.
- **Missing Seal or Stamp:** Some contracts require an official seal to be legally validated. Omitting this detail can render the contract invalid.
- **Imbalance of Rights and Obligations:** Imposing heavy obligations on one party without equivalent consideration can be deemed unbalanced and abusive.
- **Excessive Penalty Clauses:** Imposing disproportionate penalties for breaches can be illegal and difficult to

enforce.

By recognizing these frequent errors, contract drafters can take steps to avoid them, thereby improving the clarity, fairness, and legal validity of their agreements. Careful attention to detail at each stage of drafting and review is essential for creating robust and effective commercial contracts.

4.2 Identifying Legal Pitfalls

Spotting legal pitfalls in a commercial contract is crucial to ensuring its validity and protecting the interests of the involved parties. Legal pitfalls can render a contract contestable or partially unenforceable. Here are the main methods and aspects to consider when identifying and correcting these pitfalls:

Legal Compliance Analysis
Verification of Mandatory Clauses
- **Objective:** Ensure that all mandatory clauses are present and compliant with applicable laws.
- **Action:** Compare the contract with the legal and regulatory requirements of the relevant jurisdiction.

Review of Clause Validity
- **Objective:** Identify clauses that might be deemed invalid or unenforceable by a court.
- **Action:** Check whether limitation of liability, non-compete, or penalty clauses comply with legal standards.

Identification of Ambiguities and Inconsistencies
Evaluation of Ambiguous Terms
- **Objective:** Spot terms or expressions that could be interpreted in multiple ways.
- **Action:** Rephrase ambiguous clauses to make them clear and precise.

Verification of Internal Consistency
- **Objective:** Ensure that all clauses in the contract complement each other and do not contradict.
- **Action:** Compare clauses with each other to detect potential inconsistencies.

Verification of Rights and Obligations
Balancing Rights and Obligations

- **Objective:** Identify clauses that create a significant imbalance between the parties.
- **Action:** Modify unbalanced clauses to equitably distribute rights and obligations.

Review of Termination Provisions

- **Objective:** Ensure that termination conditions are clear and fair to all parties.
- **Action:** Include specific termination conditions and a reasonable notice period.

Evaluation of Protective Clauses

Data Protection and Confidentiality

- **Objective:** Ensure that confidential information and personal data are adequately protected.
- **Action:** Check that confidentiality and data protection clauses comply with current regulations such as GDPR.

Force Majeure and Unforeseen Events Clauses

- **Objective:** Cover unforeseen events that could impact contractual performance.
- **Action:** Develop a robust force majeure clause, including a clear definition of covered events.

Inclusion of Dispute Resolution Mechanisms

Dispute Resolution Procedures

- **Objective:** Specify procedures for dispute resolution to avoid prolonged and costly litigation.
- **Action:** Include mediation and arbitration clauses as alternatives to traditional court proceedings.

Competent Jurisdiction

- **Objective:** Determine which court or jurisdiction will be competent in case of a dispute.
- **Action:** Clearly specify jurisdiction in the contract.

Consultation and Validation

Expert Review

- **Objective:** Ensure that the contract has been reviewed by commercial law specialists.
- **Action:** Engage legal advisors for final review and professional validation.

Stakeholder Feedback
- **Objective:** Gather input from stakeholders on specific clauses and the overall balance of the contract.
- **Action:** Organize feedback and approval sessions to discuss sensitive points.

By following these methodical steps to identify legal pitfalls, you can draft more secure contracts that are better protected against challenges. A legally robust contract not only protects the parties but also reinforces trust and transparency in business relationships.

4.3 Solutions and Strategies to Remedy Pitfalls

Once legal pitfalls have been identified in a commercial contract, it is crucial to implement solutions and strategies to correct them. This section explores different approaches to remedy weaknesses and strengthen the legal solidity of the contract.

Clarification of Ambiguous Clauses

Redefining Terms and Expressions

- **Objective:** Eliminate any ambiguity to ensure clear and uniform interpretation.
- **Solution:** Rephrase vague or open-ended terms using precise definitions and concrete examples.

Adding Definitions

- **Objective:** Clarify the meaning of key terms in the contract.
- **Solution:** Create a dedicated definitions section at the beginning of the contract to explain the meaning of each technical term or specific jargon used.

Rebalancing Rights and Obligations

Aligning Obligations

- **Objective:** Ensure that commitments made by the parties are fair and proportionate.
- **Solution:** Review each party's obligations to ensure they are balanced, adding considerations where necessary.

Revising Liability Clauses

- **Objective:** Ensure fair distribution of liability in case of breach.
- **Solution:** Adjust liability limitation clauses to be reasonable and in line with industry practices.

Strengthening Termination Clauses

Including Specific Grounds for Termination

- **Objective:** Clearly specify situations that justify early termination.
- **Solution:** Detail termination grounds, procedures to follow, and required notices to allow proper termination.

Reasonable Notice Periods

- **Objective:** Provide sufficient time for parties to prepare for termination.
- **Solution:** Set notice periods that align with industry standards and the specific needs of the parties.

Data Protection and Confidentiality

Strengthening Confidentiality Clauses

- **Objective:** Protect sensitive and confidential information.
- **Solution:** Specify the types of information covered, each party's obligations regarding their protection, and penalties for non-compliance.

Compliance with Data Protection Regulations

- **Objective:** Ensure that the contract complies with data protection laws.
- **Solution:** Integrate specific clauses related to data protection, including the obligation to notify data breaches and the rights of data subjects.

Adoption of Verification and Validation Techniques

Use of Standardized Contract Templates

- **Objective:** Ensure compliance and effectiveness of common clauses.
- **Solution:** Adopt contract templates recommended by professional associations or legal advisors.

Incorporation of Regular Audits and Reviews

- **Objective:** Ensure that the contract remains relevant and compliant with legal developments.

- **Solution:** Implement regular audit processes to review and update contract terms as necessary.

Dispute Management and Conflict Resolution

Alternative Dispute Resolution Mechanisms

- **Objective:** Provide solutions for resolving disputes quickly and effectively.
- **Solution:** Include mediation and arbitration clauses to encourage amicable dispute resolution before resorting to court action.

Competent Jurisdiction Clause

- **Objective:** Pre-determine the competent court in case of dispute.
- **Solution:** Clearly define the competent jurisdiction in the contract based on criteria such as the location of the parties or the place of contract execution.

Use of Technological Tools

Automation of Review Processes

- **Objective:** Speed up the detection of errors and pitfalls.
- **Solution:** Use specialized contract analysis software to automatically identify problematic elements.

Collaborative Editing Platforms

- **Objective:** Facilitate collaboration between parties during contract review.
- **Solution:** Use tools like Google Docs or Microsoft Teams to enable real-time modifications and direct comments.

By applying these solutions and strategies, you can effectively correct the identified legal pitfalls in a commercial contract. A proactive approach to evaluating and improving clauses ensures the solidity, clarity, and legality of agreements, thereby strengthening trust between parties and reducing the risk of future disputes.

4.4 Practical Exercises: Reviewing and Correcting Sample Contracts

The best way to master the art of reviewing and correcting commercial contracts is by practicing with practical examples. Here are some realistic scenarios and typical contracts to help you apply the techniques and strategies discussed in the previous chapters.

Example 1: Service Agreement
Context:
- **Parties:** Alpha Consulting (Service Provider) and Beta Industries (Client)
- **Purpose:** Provision of strategic consulting services for a duration of six months.

Initial Clause to Revise:
- **Confidentiality Clause:** "Information exchanged between the parties during the contract period must be treated as confidential."

Identified Pitfalls:
- **Vague and Generalized:** The clause does not specify which information is considered confidential or the duration of confidentiality after the contract ends.

Proposed Correction:
- "The parties agree that all technical, commercial, and strategic information exchanged under this contract is considered confidential. Each party undertakes not to disclose this information to third parties without the prior written consent of the other party, for the duration of the contract and for a period of two years following its termination."

Objective:
- Clarify the types of information covered and the duration of confidentiality.

Example 2: Sales Contract

Context:
- **Parties:** Gamma Equipments (Seller) and Delta Corp (Buyer)
- **Purpose:** Sale and delivery of industrial machinery.

Initial Clause to Revise:
- **Delivery Clause:** "The machines will be delivered as soon as possible after the contract is signed."

Identified Pitfalls:
- **Lack of Precision:** The clause is vague and does not define a clear delivery deadline.

Proposed Correction:
- "The machines will be delivered to the buyer's address within 30 calendar days from the date of signing this contract. In case of delay, the seller undertakes to inform the buyer as soon as possible and to propose a new delivery date."

Objective:
- Provide a specific delivery deadline and a procedure in case of delay.

Example 3: Distribution Agreement

Context:
- **Parties:** Epsilon Products (Supplier) and Zeta Distributions (Distributor)
- **Purpose:** Exclusive distribution of electronic products in a specific region.

Initial Clause to Revise:
- **Automatic Renewal Clause:** "This contract will automatically renew for an additional one-year term unless either party notifies its intent not to renew at least 10 days before the contract's end."

Identified Pitfalls:

- **Too Short Notice Period:** Ten days is insufficient time to prepare for termination or renegotiation.

Proposed Correction:

- "This contract will automatically renew for an additional one-year term unless either party notifies its intent not to renew at least 60 days before the end of the current contractual period."

Objective:

- Extend the notice period to allow ample preparation.

Example 4: License Agreement

Context:

- **Parties:** Theta Software (Licensor) and Iota Solutions (Licensee)
- **Purpose:** Software usage license for a specified duration.

Initial Clause to Revise:

- **Warranty Clause:** "The licensor guarantees that the software is free of defects."

Identified Pitfalls:

- **Too General and Unrealistic:** Any absolute guarantee is difficult to maintain legally.

Proposed Correction:

- "The licensor guarantees that the software will substantially function according to the provided documentation for a period of 12 months from the date of delivery. In the event of a substantial defect during this period, the licensor undertakes to correct the defect at no additional cost to the licensee."

Objective:

- Limit the warranty to a specific period and define what constitutes a substantial defect.

By practicing these exercises, you can improve your skills in reviewing and correcting commercial contracts, strengthening your expertise and confidence in drafting robust contractual documents that comply with professional and legal standards.

CHAPTER 5: CONTRACT NEGOTIATION

After learning how to spot and correct flaws in contracts, the next step is mastering the art of negotiation. A well-conducted negotiation allows for the conclusion of fair and beneficial agreements for all parties involved. In this chapter, we will explore negotiation techniques and best practices to achieve favorable outcomes.

5.1 Basic Principles of Negotiation

Negotiation is a complex art that rests on several fundamental principles. Mastering these principles helps achieve balanced and lasting agreements. Here are the main basic principles of negotiation in the context of commercial contracts:

Mutual Understanding

Active Listening

- **Principle:** Listen carefully to the other party to understand their needs, concerns, and motivations.
- **Application:** Practice active listening by rephrasing important points, asking clarifying questions, and showing empathy.

Clear Communication

- **Principle:** Use clear and precise language to avoid misunderstandings.
- **Application:** Express your own needs and requirements directly, while remaining respectful and open to the other party's suggestions.

Solid Preparation

Research and Analysis

- **Principle:** Arrive well-prepared with a thorough understanding of the contract details and the interests of all parties.
- **Application:** Gather information on the industry, the parties' backgrounds, competitive positions, and relevant legal precedents.

Goal Setting

- **Principle:** Clearly define the primary and secondary objectives you wish to achieve in the negotiation.
- **Application:** Set realistic and prioritized goals, as well as non-negotiable points and areas of flexibility.

Flexibility and Adaptability

Compromise and Flexibility
- **Principle:** Be ready to make compromises and adapt your position based on the progress of the negotiation.
- **Application:** Identify possible concessions and acceptable alternatives to mutually satisfy the needs of the parties.

Conflict Management
- **Principle:** Manage disagreements constructively to avoid deadlocks.
- **Application:** Use conflict resolution techniques such as mediation, and remain calm and factual during tense discussions.

Value Creation

Win-Win Approach
- **Principle:** Seek to create solutions that benefit all parties involved.
- **Application:** Identify common interests and explore innovative options that add value for everyone.

Innovation and Creativity
- **Principle:** Think creatively to find innovative solutions to sticking points.
- **Application:** Consider conditional concessions, performance clauses, success bonuses, or other instruments to enrich the agreement.

Maintaining Good Relationships

Respect and Politeness
- **Principle:** Treat the other party with respect to build a trusting relationship.
- **Application:** Avoid personal attacks, value opposing viewpoints, and maintain a positive attitude.

Commitment and Reliability
- **Principle:** Show commitment to agreements and

demonstrate reliability.
- **Application:** Keep your promises, follow up regularly on commitments, and maintain open communication even after the negotiation.

Strategic Management
Timing and Opportunities

- **Principle:** Use timing to your advantage to optimize negotiation results.
- **Application:** Know when to speed up or slow down discussions, and choose the right moments to present proposals or make concessions.

Anticipation of Objections

- **Principle:** Anticipate objections and potential barriers to be ready to respond effectively.
- **Application:** Prepare strong counterarguments and supporting facts to overcome objections as they arise.

By integrating these basic principles into your negotiation approach, you will be better equipped to conduct productive discussions and reach solid contractual agreements that benefit all parties. Mastering these fundamentals is essential for successfully navigating the commercial negotiation process.

5.2 Preparation and Goal Setting

Preparation is a crucial element for successful negotiation. A well-prepared negotiator anticipates needs, contingencies, and potentialities to navigate effectively through the discussions. The preparation process involves several important steps, including thorough analysis and clear goal setting. Here's how to properly prepare and establish goals for a commercial contract negotiation.

Preliminary Analysis

Research and Information Gathering

- **Objective:** Gather all relevant information about the parties involved, the negotiation context, and previous contractual agreements.
- **Action:** Study the industry, stakeholder history, their motivations, needs, and vulnerabilities. Use reliable sources such as financial reports, market studies, and industry publications.

SWOT Analysis

- **Objective:** Identify the strengths, weaknesses, opportunities, and threats of the situation.
- **Action:** Evaluate your own strengths and weaknesses, as well as those of the other party. Identify common opportunities and potential threats to the success of the negotiation.

Defining the Stakes

- **Objective:** Assess what is truly at stake for each party.
- **Action:** Define the financial, legal, strategic, and relational stakes. Prioritize these stakes to have a clear vision of what is essential and what can be negotiated.

Goal Setting

Identifying Primary and Secondary Goals

- **Objective:** Distinguish what is absolutely necessary from what would be beneficial to obtain.

- **Action:** Establish a list of primary, non-negotiable goals and secondary, desirable but compromise-able goals. For example, a primary goal could be securing a strict non-disclosure clause, while a secondary goal might be obtaining more favorable payment terms.

SMART Objectives

- **Objective:** Ensure that goals are clear and achievable.
- **Action:** Formulate your goals according to the SMART model: Specific, Measurable, Achievable, Realistic, and Time-bound. For example, "Obtain a 10% reduction in supply costs within 30 days of signing the contract."

Strategic Preparation

Scenario Development

- **Objective:** Prepare different possible scenarios and appropriate responses.
- **Action:** Create "what-if" scenarios for each key negotiation point. For example, what will happen if the other party refuses a crucial concession? Prepare counter-proposals in advance.

Developing a BATNA (Best Alternative to a Negotiated Agreement)

- **Objective:** Determine the best alternative if the negotiation fails.
- **Action:** Identify and prepare for the best alternative available if an agreement cannot be reached. For example, having another potential supplier ready can serve as leverage in negotiations with the current supplier.

Setting Limits and Concessions

- **Objective:** Know how far you are willing to go and what you are willing to give up.
- **Action:** Define clear limits for each negotiation point and prepare a list of possible concessions that do not

affect your primary goals.

Logistical Preparation

Document Organization

- **Objective:** Have all necessary documents available and ordered.
- **Action:** Prepare a complete file with previous contract versions, all correspondence, meeting notes, and any other relevant documents for quick reference.

Negotiation Team Preparation

- **Objective:** Ensure that all team members are aligned and well-informed.
- **Action:** Brief each team member on the goals, strategies, and expected roles. Ensure everyone is thoroughly familiar with the points to be addressed and possible concessions.

Timing Management

- **Objective:** Optimize timelines for effective negotiation.
- **Action:** Establish a clear schedule with deadlines for each stage of the negotiation. Plan breaks to reassess the situation and adjust strategies if necessary.

Psychological Preparation

Mental Preparation

- **Objective:** Mentally prepare to remain calm and focused.
- **Action:** Adopt relaxation and visualization techniques, anticipate difficulties, and prepare to maintain a positive and resilient attitude.

Anticipating Adverse Tactics

- **Objective:** Foresee the other party's strategies and be ready to react.
- **Action:** Consider potential tactics from the other party (e.g., bluffing or pressure tactics) and prepare strategic responses for each situation.

By implementing these preparation and goal-setting steps, you can enter a negotiation with a clear vision and a well-defined strategy. The key is to remain flexible while having well-established goals and limits, increasing the chances of reaching a beneficial agreement for all parties.

5.3 Negotiation Techniques

A successful negotiation relies on the use of appropriate techniques that allow for effective and productive discussions. Here are some proven techniques to help you navigate the negotiation process and reach satisfactory agreements for all parties:

Active Listening Technique

- **Objective:** Fully understand the needs and concerns of the other party.
- **Application:** Practice active listening by rephrasing what the other party has said, asking open-ended questions to clarify points, and showing empathy. For example, "If I understand correctly, you are concerned about delivery timelines. Can you tell me more about what specifically worries you?"

BATNA (Best Alternative to a Negotiated Agreement) Technique

- **Objective:** Strengthen your position by knowing your best alternatives if the negotiation fails.
- **Application:** Clearly identify your BATNA before starting discussions. Use this knowledge to evaluate offers during negotiations and to have a solid base if you need to walk away from the negotiation table.

Strategic Questioning Technique

- **Objective:** Deeply explore the other party's positions without appearing too interrogative.
- **Application:** Ask strategic questions that encourage the other party to reveal their needs and motivations. For example, "What are your main goals for this project?" or "How do you see our collaboration evolving in the long term?"

Anchoring Technique

- **Objective:** Influence the discussion by setting a starting point for negotiations.

- **Application:** Start negotiations with an ambitious but reasonable initial offer or request that will steer discussions in your direction. For example, propose an initial price slightly higher to allow room for later concessions.

Reciprocal Concessions Technique

- **Objective:** Create a sense of fairness and reciprocity in negotiations.
- **Application:** When you concede something to the other party, ask for an equivalent concession in return. For example, "If we agree to extend the warranty period, would you be willing to shorten the payment terms?"

Silence Technique

- **Objective:** Give the other party time to think and potentially reveal additional information.
- **Application:** After asking a question or making a proposal, remain silent and let the other party respond. Use silence as a tool to show that you expect a serious and thoughtful response.

Repetition Technique

- **Objective:** Ensure clarity and mutual understanding.
- **Application:** Repeat or rephrase key points in the discussion to ensure all parties are on the same page. For example, "To be sure we agree, you confirm that deliveries will start on June 1st, correct?"

Partition Technique

- **Objective:** Break down complex issues to find partial solutions.
- **Application:** When blockages occur, divide the issues into smaller, more manageable elements. For example, if financial terms are problematic, discuss price, payment terms, and potential discounts separately.

Quid Pro Quo Technique
- **Objective:** Exchange items of equivalent value to progress toward an agreement.
- **Application:** Propose exchanges where each party receives something important to them. For example, "We can agree to your request for product modification, provided you extend the contract by an additional year."

Scenario Visualization Technique
- **Objective:** Anticipate the potential consequences of different offers and counteroffers.
- **Application:** Discuss possible scenarios for each proposal and jointly evaluate their short- and long-term impacts. Use charts or matrices to illustrate the advantages and disadvantages of each option.

Application of Techniques

Real-Life Case Studies
- **Application:** Apply these techniques to real or fictional case studies to practice their use in various situations.
- **Action:** Organize simulation negotiation sessions to reinforce these skills in a group setting.

Follow-Up and Adjustments
- **Objective:** Evaluate the techniques used after each negotiation to determine what worked and what could be improved.
- **Action:** Adapt and refine your techniques based on feedback and results obtained.

Continuous Learning
- **Objective:** Expand and diversify your negotiation techniques by participating in training and reading specialized literature.

By integrating these techniques into your negotiations, you can improve your ability to achieve strong and satisfactory agreements for all parties. A strategic and well-structured approach facilitates managing discussions, effectively resolving conflicts, and building mutually beneficial agreements.

5.4 Negotiating Sensitive Clauses

Certain clauses in commercial contracts often cause friction and require special attention during negotiations. It is crucial to approach these sensitive clauses with a specific strategy to ensure a balanced agreement. Here are the techniques and considerations to effectively negotiate sensitive clauses:

Compliance and Liability Clauses

- **Objective:** Clearly define the responsibilities and obligations of the parties in case of non-compliance or default.
- **Strategy:**
    - **Clarity and Precision:** Draft precise clauses detailing the conditions of compliance and associated responsibilities.
    - **Documented Justification:** Use case studies or legal precedents to justify your liability requirements.
    - **Limitation of Liability:** Propose reasonable limits on financial liability to avoid disproportionate penalties.

Payment and Penalty Clauses

- **Objective:** Set fair payment terms and proportionate penalties.
- **Strategy:**
    - **Clear Payment Terms:** Clearly define deadlines, accepted payment methods, and discounts for early payments.
    - **Reasonable Penalties:** Negotiate penalties with practical considerations for late or missed payments, taking into account the financial capacities of the parties.
    - **Flexibility:** Provide options for rescheduling or

grace periods in case of temporary financial difficulties.

Non-Compete and Exclusivity Clauses

- **Objective:** Protect commercial interests without excessively restricting the parties' freedoms.
- **Strategy:**
    - **Duration and Scope:** Limit the duration and geographic scope of non-compete clauses to ensure their acceptability and legal compliance.
    - **Reciprocity:** Ensure that non-compete commitments are mutual and fair.
    - **Compensation:** Propose compensation in exchange for the imposed restrictions to make the clause more acceptable.

Duration and Termination Clauses

- **Objective:** Facilitate the continuation of the contractual relationship while allowing for equitable exits if necessary.
- **Strategy:**
    - **Precision on Duration:** Clearly establish the initial contract duration and renewal conditions.
    - **Termination Conditions:** Define clear and fair termination grounds with reasonable notice periods.
    - **Termination Indemnities:** Provide for termination indemnities to compensate for specific investments and incurred costs.

Confidentiality Clauses

- **Objective:** Protect sensitive information while allowing for some operational flexibility.
- **Strategy:**
    - **Specificity:** Specifically identify what

information is considered confidential.
- **Confidentiality Duration:** Limit the confidentiality duration to a realistic and justifiable period post-contract.
- **Exclusions:** Include clear exceptions for information already public or independently obtained.

Intellectual Property Clauses

- **Objective:** Protect intellectual property rights while allowing increased use by the parties.
- **Strategy:**
  - **Broad Definition:** Clearly define what constitutes intellectual property covered by the contract.
  - **License and Usage:** Establish clearly defined usage conditions and negotiate balanced licenses.
  - **Protection and Defense:** Provide mechanisms for protection and responsibilities in case of infringement.

Force Majeure Clauses

- **Objective:** Manage risks related to unforeseen events in an equitable manner.
- **Strategy:**
  - **Key Definition:** Establish a clear definition of force majeure events covered by the clause.
  - **Notification Obligations:** Provide for prompt notification obligations of force majeure events.
  - **Suspension and Termination:** Determine the parties' rights and obligations during the suspension of obligations and the conditions for termination in the event of prolonged force majeure.

Dispute Resolution Clauses
- **Objective:** Provide effective mechanisms to resolve conflicts equitably and efficiently.
- **Strategy:**
  - **Mediation and Arbitration:** Favor alternative dispute resolution methods before resorting to litigation.
  - **Venue and Jurisdiction:** Mutually agree on the venue and jurisdiction competent in case of disputes.
  - **Duration and Costs:** Provide for deadlines for conflict resolution and an equitable distribution of associated costs.

Automatic Renewal Clauses
- **Objective:** Manage contract renewals predictably and consensually.
- **Strategy:**
  - **Renewal Conditions:** Specify the conditions and notifications necessary for the automatic renewal of the contract.
  - **Audit Periods:** Provide for evaluation periods before renewal dates to allow for adjustments to terms as needed.

By negotiating these sensitive clauses with a strategic and pragmatic approach, you can ensure a more stable and balanced contractual relationship. Thorough preparation, clear communication, and equitable concessions are essential to achieving lasting and satisfactory agreements for all parties.

5.5 The Art of Compromise

Compromise is a central component of any successful negotiation. The art of compromise involves finding solutions that, while not ideal for one party, are acceptable to all parties involved and contribute to establishing a balanced agreement. Here's how to master the art of compromise in commercial contract negotiations:

Understanding Priorities

Identifying Priorities

- **Objective:** Identify the absolute and secondary priorities of each party.
- **Action:** Rank your goals according to importance and encourage the other party to do the same. For example, product quality may be a top priority for the buyer, while price may be secondary.

Non-Negotiable Points

- **Objective:** Determine the non-negotiable elements for each party.
- **Action:** Clarify early in the negotiation the points on which you cannot compromise, and ask the other party to do the same.

Balancing Concessions and Gains

Concession Analysis

- **Objective:** Evaluate the impact of concessions on overall party satisfaction.
- **Action:** For each concession made, ensure that it brings a proportional gain. For example, agreeing to slightly longer delivery times in exchange for a reduced price.

Reciprocity Principle

- **Objective:** Ensure fairness in concessions made.
- **Action:** For each concession granted, ask for a counter-concession that balances the value of the

initial concession. This maintains fairness and shows your willingness to cooperate while protecting your interests.

Compromise Techniques

Multiple Options

- **Objective:** Offer multiple options to facilitate compromise.
- **Action:** Propose two or three viable alternatives regarding a negotiation point. For example, offering a price reduction for a larger purchase volume or extending the warranty in exchange for a longer agreement.

Step-by-Step Negotiation

- **Objective:** Facilitate compromises by proceeding in stages.
- **Action:** Break the negotiations into steps or phases, starting with the easiest points to resolve to establish trust, then addressing more complex issues.

Room for Maneuver

- **Objective:** Keep room for maneuver to facilitate exchanges.
- **Action:** Identify possible room for maneuver in your positions without sacrificing your essential priorities, and use these margins to negotiate.

Managing Emotions and Perception

Emotion and Objectivity

- **Objective:** Maintain an emotionally neutral and objective approach.
- **Action:** Stay calm and factual, even when the other party expresses strong emotions. Use stress management techniques to stay focused on common interests.

Perception of Concessions

- **Objective:** Properly value the concessions made.
- **Action:** Present each concession as a constructive contribution to the overall solution, not as a weakness. Highlight the long-term benefits of accepted compromises.

Creativity in Solutions

Innovation and Originality

- **Objective:** Find creative solutions that meet both parties' needs.
- **Action:** Think outside the box to find innovative arrangements. For example, incorporating periodic review clauses to adjust terms according to market developments.

Flexible Approaches

- **Objective:** Stay open to adjustments and alternatives.
- **Action:** Adopt a flexible approach in conflict resolution by exploring temporary arrangements or hybrid solutions.

Strengthening Relationships

Mutual Trust and Respect

- **Objective:** Build and maintain a relationship of trust and respect.
- **Action:** Be transparent in your communications, honor commitments, and be responsive to the other party's needs. Mutual trust facilitates compromise.

Long-Term Commitment

- **Objective:** Look beyond the immediate agreement to consider future benefits.
- **Action:** View compromises as investments in a long-term relationship. For example, accepting slightly less favorable terms in the short term to strengthen collaboration on future projects.

By adopting these strategies and techniques to excel in the art of compromise, you can successfully navigate complex negotiations and reach balanced agreements. The ability to make thoughtful concessions while protecting your key interests is essential for building sustainable and fruitful commercial partnerships.

5.6 Negotiation Simulations

Negotiation simulations are valuable tools for developing and refining negotiation skills. They allow for the recreation of real-world scenarios in a controlled environment, offering an opportunity for practical learning. Here's how to structure and effectively use negotiation simulations to improve your skills.

Preparing the Simulation

Scenario Selection

- **Objective:** Select realistic and relevant scenarios for the participants.
- **Action:** Choose common negotiation situations in your field, such as negotiating service contracts, distribution agreements, or partnerships.

Role Assignment

- **Objective:** Assign specific roles to participants to reflect a real situation.
- **Action:** Assign each participant a precise role, such as a supplier, client, intermediary, or lawyer. Provide them with detailed role descriptions and each party's objectives.

Setting Objectives

- **Objective:** Establish clear objectives for each party involved.
- **Action:** Define explicit objectives for each role, along with non-negotiable points and secondary goals. For example, a supplier might want a quick payment clause, while a client might insist on strict delivery deadlines.

Conducting the Simulation

Opening Phase

- **Objective:** Initiate the discussion and establish a negotiation framework.
- **Action:** Start with formal introductions and invite each

party to present their initial goals and expectations. Establish negotiation rules, such as active listening and mutual respect.

Discussion Phase

- **Objective:** Explore each party's positions and identify points of convergence and divergence.
- **Action:** Encourage participants to exchange proposals, ask questions, and rephrase points to ensure mutual understanding. Promote the use of negotiation techniques covered earlier, such as anchoring and strategic questioning.

Negotiation Phase

- **Objective:** Exchange offers and counteroffers to reach compromises.
- **Action:** Engage participants in the exchange of concessions and counter-offers. Spend time on sensitive clauses, using techniques like partition and multiple options to find acceptable solutions for all parties.

Finalization Phase

- **Objective:** Conclude the negotiation with a formal agreement.
- **Action:** Draft a summary of the agreement reached, including the negotiated terms and commitments made by each party. Ensure that all parties sign this summary to confirm their agreement.

Debriefing and Analysis

Reflection and Feedback

- **Objective:** Encourage participants to reflect on their performance and the results of the simulation.
- **Action:** Organize a debriefing session where each participant can share their impressions and learnings. Ask questions like "What did you find most challenging?" and "What aspects of your approach

worked well?"

Strategy Analysis
- **Objective:** Analyze the strategies used and their effectiveness.
- **Action:** Review the negotiation strategies deployed and discuss their effectiveness. Identify techniques that led to positive results and those that encountered obstacles.

Recommendations for Improvement
- **Objective:** Provide practical advice for improving negotiation skills.
- **Action:** Offer constructive suggestions for each participant, such as alternative techniques to try or specific areas to work on, like stress management or improving clear communication.

Integration into Training Programs

Educational Modules
- **Objective:** Integrate negotiation simulations into ongoing training programs.
- **Action:** Create specific modules dedicated to negotiation simulations, with exercises tailored to participants' skill levels. Use varied scenarios to cover different aspects of contract negotiation.

Repetition and Refinement
- **Objective:** Allow for regular practice and continuous improvement.
- **Action:** Organize regular simulation sessions to allow participants to practice and refine their skills. Assess progress and adjust scenarios to address new challenges and complexities.

By integrating negotiation simulations into your training process, you can significantly improve participants' skills, enabling them to engage in real negotiations with greater confidence and effectiveness. Simulations provide a dynamic and interactive learning environment that helps develop the analytical, strategic, and interpersonal skills essential for successful commercial negotiations.

CHAPTER 6: FORMALIZATION AND MONITORING OF CONTRACTS

Once the contract is negotiated and signed, it is crucial to know how to manage any disputes that may arise. Proactive conflict management helps minimize disruptions and maintain healthy business relationships. In the next chapter, we will discuss different approaches to dispute resolution and the management of contractual disagreements.

6.1 Formalization of a Revised Contract

The formalization of a revised contract is a crucial step that officially confirms the agreement between the parties. It ensures that all modifications made are correctly integrated and that the final document is legally binding. Here's how to effectively and rigorously formalize a revised contract:

Integration of Modifications
- **Consolidation of Changes**
  - **Objective:** Integrate all modifications made during negotiations into a single document.
  - **Action:** Combine all validated revisions into a final version of the contract. Ensure that the modifications are properly integrated and clearly visible, using track changes tools in word processing software.
- **Verification of Internal References**
  - **Objective:** Ensure the consistency and accuracy of internal references (sections, articles, annexes).
  - **Action:** Review all internal references to ensure they point to the correct sections. Correct any identified inconsistencies.

Final Review
- **Complete Reading**
  - **Objective:** Perform a final read-through to verify the clarity and precision of each clause.
  - **Action:** Read the entire contract to ensure all clauses are clear, well-written, and easily understood by all involved parties.
- **Double-Check Details**
  - **Objective:** Ensure that all essential details

(names, dates, amounts, etc.) are correct.
- **Action:** Carefully review the names of the parties, dates, financial amounts, and all other sensitive data to confirm their accuracy.

Legal Certification

- **Consultation with Legal Advisors**
  - **Objective:** Obtain legal validation of the revised contract.
  - **Action:** Have the contract reviewed by legal advisors to ensure its compliance with applicable laws and regulations. Incorporate legal recommendations into the final version.
- **Compliance Verification**
  - **Objective:** Ensure compliance with sector-specific laws and local regulations.
  - **Action:** Perform a compliance check to ensure the contract meets all legal requirements specific to your sector and jurisdiction.

Signing and Execution

- **Preparation of Signed Copies**
  - **Objective:** Prepare the final copies of the contract for signature by all parties.
  - **Action:** Print several copies of the contract or use a recognized electronic signature service to prepare the digital document for signatures.
- **Obtaining Signatures**
  - **Objective:** Obtain the official signatures of all involved parties.
  - **Action:** Organize a signing meeting or use electronic signature tools to collect signatures on all copies of the contract. Ensure all parties sign the necessary pages and initial significant changes if required.

Archiving and Distribution
- **Physical and Digital Archiving**
    - **Objective:** Store the signed contract in secure archives.
    - **Action:** Archive the signed copies of the contract in a secure physical storage space and scan them for digital storage in a protected electronic document management system.
- **Distribution of Copies**
    - **Objective:** Distribute copies of the signed contract to all concerned parties.
    - **Action:** Send a signed copy of the contract to each key stakeholder and ensure they acknowledge receipt.

Documentation of Interactions
- **Recording Modifications**
    - **Objective:** Maintain a detailed history of all modifications made.
    - **Action:** Keep a log of all revisions and modifications made, including the dates of changes, justifications, and approvals received.
- **Traceability**
    - **Objective:** Ensure the traceability of interactions and decisions.
    - **Action:** Document all key interactions and decisions made during the formalization process. Use reports and meeting memos to capture this information.

By applying these principles, you can ensure that the revised contract is properly formalized, compliant with legal requirements, and ready for execution.

6.2 Clear and Precise Language

Drafting a contract with clear and precise language is crucial to avoid misunderstandings and ensure that all parties fully understand the terms and conditions of the agreement. Clear communication facilitates the execution of the contract and reduces the risk of disputes. Here are the keys to writing contract clauses effectively and intelligibly:

Use of Defined Terms

- **Define Technical Terms**
    - **Objective:** Ensure that technical terms or specific jargon are understood by all parties.
    - **Action:** Include a definitions section at the beginning of the contract where all technical terms are clearly defined. For example, "'Service' refers to any activity provided by the Provider as defined in Annex A."
- **Clarity of References**
    - **Objective:** Avoid ambiguities by using consistently defined terms.
    - **Action:** Refer to defined terms consistently throughout the contract. Use the exact same term for the same concept without variation.

Syntax and Structure

- **Short and Simple Sentences**
    - **Objective:** Facilitate understanding by using short sentences and a simple structure.
    - **Action:** Limit sentence length and use a subject-verb-object structure. For example, instead of "The Buyer, upon receipt of the goods delivered by the Seller, must immediately verify the conformity of said goods...," prefer "The Buyer must verify the conformity of the goods

immediately after receipt."
- **Avoidance of Multiple Negatives**
    - **Objective:** Avoid confusion caused by multiple negatives.
    - **Action:** Use positive affirmations. For example, replace "The products cannot be returned unless the non-conformity is not disputed" with "The products can only be returned if the non-conformity is confirmed."

Precision of Clauses
- **Detail Obligations**
    - **Objective:** Make each party's obligations exhaustive and specific.
    - **Action:** Describe precisely the actions expected of each party, including deadlines and performance criteria. For example, "The Provider must deliver the services described in Annex B within 30 days following the contract signing."
- **Avoid Ambiguities**
    - **Objective:** Prevent multiple interpretations of clauses.
    - **Action:** Avoid vague terms like "reasonable," "sufficient," or "necessary" without defining them. For example, replace "within a reasonable time" with "within 15 calendar days."

Consistency and Repetitions
- **Terminological Consistency**
    - **Objective:** Use the same terms throughout the document for the same concept.
    - **Action:** Once a term is chosen, use it consistently without synonyms. For example, if you use "Contract" to refer to the agreement, do

not replace it with "Agreement" in another part of the document.

- **Moderate Use of Repetitions**
    - **Objective:** Avoid unnecessary repetitions that can clutter the text.
    - **Action:** Group similar information to avoid repeating the same clauses in different sections. Use internal references sparingly to direct the reader to additional clauses without redundancy.

Adapted Legal Language

- **Avoid Excessive Jargon**
    - **Objective:** Use legal language only when necessary and make it understandable.
    - **Action:** Replace complex jargon with simpler terms when possible. For example, instead of "hereinafter referred to," use "hereafter called."

- **Explicit Legal Markers**
    - **Objective:** Ensure clear delineation of legal obligations.
    - **Action:** Use explicit legal markers to indicate obligations and legal restrictions, such as "In accordance with Article 123 of the Civil Code."

Verification and Revisions

- **Proofreading and Editing**
    - **Objective:** Ensure the clarity and accuracy of the language used.
    - **Action:** Proofread the contract multiple times, ideally by different people, to verify its interpretability. Use grammatical and linguistic verification tools to identify errors and ambiguities.

- **Comprehension Test**

- **Objective:** Verify understanding by someone external to the negotiations.
- **Action:** Have the contract read by someone who did not participate in its drafting to confirm that the language is clear and understandable. Note their questions and adjust the language accordingly.

By applying these principles of clear and precise drafting, you can create contracts that are easily understood by all stakeholders, thus reducing the risk of misunderstandings and disputes. Simple but legally relevant language contributes to the transparency and feasibility of contractual agreements.

6.3 Legal Validation and Approval

Legal validation and approval are essential steps to ensure that the revised contract is legally binding and compliant with applicable laws and regulations. This phase secures the agreement and prevents future disputes. Here are the main steps to follow to legally validate and obtain approval for a revised contract:

Consultation with Legal Advisors
- **Internal Legal Review**
  - **Objective:** Conduct an initial legal review within the company.
  - **Action:** Submit the revised contract to the internal legal team, if applicable, for a first review. The team should verify compliance with internal policies and basic legal standards.
- **Analysis by External Experts**
  - **Objective:** Obtain independent and specialized validation.
  - **Action:** Engage an external legal advisor or law firm specializing in commercial law to conduct a thorough analysis. The expert should verify the legality of each clause, especially regarding regulatory and sectoral compliance.

Compliance Verification
- **Compliance with Local and International Laws**
  - **Objective:** Ensure that the contract complies with all applicable laws.
  - **Action:** Review the contract to verify its compliance with the local laws of the jurisdiction where it will be executed, as well as any relevant international legislation.
- **Data Protection and Confidentiality**
  - **Objective:** Ensure compliance with data

protection regulations.
- **Action:** Check that the data protection and confidentiality clauses comply with regulations such as the GDPR for entities operating in Europe. Ensure that the provisions are adequate to protect sensitive data.

Compliance with Industry Standards
- **Sector-Specific Standards**
  - **Objective:** Align with the practices and requirements specific to your industry.
  - **Action:** Integrate recommendations from professional associations or regulatory bodies in your sector. For example, for contracts in the construction sector, comply with specific safety standards and insurance obligations.
- **Standardized Clauses**
  - **Objective:** Use standardized clauses for common issues.
  - **Action:** Use industry-recognized standard clauses for common aspects of the contract, such as liability or termination clauses, to ensure increased compliance with industry practices.

Approval Process
- **Review by Stakeholders**
  - **Objective:** Obtain approval and feedback from internal stakeholders.
  - **Action:** Share the revised contract with various stakeholders within your organization (finance, operations, risk management) for comprehensive feedback. Collect and incorporate relevant comments.
- **Collection of Formal Approvals**

- **Objective:** Obtain official approval from all parties.
- **Action:** Prepare a formal approval document for each stakeholder to sign, confirming their agreement with the content and terms of the contract. This step may involve validation meetings with key decision-makers.

Documentation and Archiving

- **Recording Approvals**
  - **Objective:** Document all approvals obtained for future reference.
  - **Action:** Record all validations and approvals in writing, including email exchanges and meeting minutes.
- **Legal Archiving**
  - **Objective:** Keep a copy of all validation and approval documents.
  - **Action:** Archive all documents related to legal validation and approvals in a secure and easily accessible location. Ensure these documents are protected from loss and accessible when needed.

Contract Management System

- **Implementation of a Contract Management System**
  - **Objective:** Effectively manage signed contracts and their approvals.
  - **Action:** Use contract management software to track approval, execution, and ongoing compliance of contracts. This system should include alerts for important deadlines and renewals.
- **Training and Awareness**
  - **Objective:** Train staff on the importance of legal

validation and approval.
- **Action:** Organize regular training sessions to raise awareness among staff about the critical steps of legal validation and the importance of obtaining the necessary approvals to ensure full compliance.

By following these rigorous steps to legally validate and approve a revised contract, you can ensure that the agreement is legally sound, balanced, and compliant with regulatory requirements. This contributes to smooth execution and protects the interests of all involved parties.

6.4 Monitoring and Updating Contracts

Monitoring and updating contracts are essential processes to ensure that agreements remain relevant, compliant, and advantageous in the long term. Proactive contract management allows for the detection and correction of potential issues before they lead to negative consequences. Here's how to implement effective monitoring and regular contract updating practices:

Establishment of a Monitoring System
- **Contract Management System (CMS)**
    - **Objective:** Centralize and automate contract monitoring.
    - **Action:** Implement contract management software (CMS) that allows for the storage, organization, and tracking of all contracts in one place. Key features include deadline alerts, renewal reminders, and compliance tracking.
- **Centralized Database**
    - **Objective:** Facilitate access to and management of contracts.
    - **Action:** Create a centralized database or repository to store all electronic and physical copies of contracts. Ensure that this database is secure and accessible only to authorized personnel.

Continuous Monitoring
- **Deadline Calendar**
    - **Objective:** Avoid missing key dates for contract review, renewal, or termination.
    - **Action:** Maintain a calendar of deadlines with automatic alerts for important dates such as renewals, performance audits, and annual

reviews.

- **Performance Tracking**
  - **Objective:** Assess the compliance and effectiveness of the contract during its execution.
  - **Action:** Implement key performance indicators (KPIs) to monitor contractual obligations and evaluate the performance of parties. For example, track delivery dates, product/service quality, and payment deadlines.

Updating Contracts

- **Periodic Audits**
  - **Objective:** Verify contract compliance and effectiveness at regular intervals.
  - **Action:** Schedule periodic audits to review each contract in execution. Identify obsolete clauses, ambiguities, and needs for revision. Document findings and necessary corrective actions.
- **Annual Reviews**
  - **Objective:** Ensure the contract remains aligned with the organization's objectives and regulatory changes.
  - **Action:** Conduct an annual review of contracts to verify their current relevance. Consider changes in laws, industry shifts, and internal company transformations that may affect the contract.

Modification Process

- **Modification Procedures**
  - **Objective:** Facilitate contract modifications in a structured and approved manner.
  - **Action:** Establish clear procedures for contract modifications, including documentation of

proposed changes, necessary approvals, and updating of official contract versions.

- **Documentation of Modifications**
    - **Objective:** Ensure traceability and transparency of modifications made.
    - **Action:** Keep a log of modifications for each contract, indicating the nature of the changes, reasons, and parties responsible for approval. Archive all revised versions and approval documents.

Risk Management and Compliance

- **Regulatory Compliance Monitoring**
    - **Objective:** Maintain compliance with constantly evolving regulations.
    - **Action:** Ensure continuous regulatory monitoring to identify new laws and regulations that could affect ongoing contracts. Modify contracts accordingly to remain in compliance.
- **Risk Management Plan**
    - **Objective:** Anticipate and manage potential risks related to contracts.
    - **Action:** Develop a risk management plan specific to contracts, including the identification of potential risks, evaluation of their impact, and implementation of mitigation strategies.

Communication and Collaboration

- **Information Sharing**
    - **Objective:** Facilitate transparent communication among all stakeholders.
    - **Action:** Establish clear and regular communication channels to share information

on contract progress, audits, and revisions. Use collaborative platforms for discussions and real-time updates.

- **Continuous Training**
  - **Objective:** Train team members on best contract management practices.
  - **Action:** Offer continuous training sessions on contract management, including the use of management software, legal review, and updating procedures.

Evaluation and Improvement

- **Contract Performance Reviews**
  - **Objective:** Evaluate the overall effectiveness of your contract management practices.
  - **Action:** Conduct periodic evaluations of contract performance to identify strengths and areas for improvement. Adjust your processes based on feedback and lessons learned.
- **Stakeholder Feedback**
  - **Objective:** Gather constructive feedback from stakeholders to improve processes.
  - **Action:** Organize feedback sessions with internal and external stakeholders to discuss potential improvements. Integrate these suggestions to refine monitoring and updating practices.

By following these methodical steps for monitoring and updating contracts, you can ensure that your agreements stay aligned with organizational goals and legal requirements. Proactive and regular contract management contributes to the stability of business relationships and the minimization of risks related to contract execution.

6.5 Dispute and Conflict Management

Dispute and conflict management is an essential component of contract management. Disagreements can arise at any time during the life of a contract, so it is crucial to have strategies and procedures in place to resolve them effectively and equitably. Here are the key steps and best practices for managing disputes and conflicts in commercial contracts:

Early Conflict Identification

- **Continuous Monitoring**
    - **Objective:** Detect early signs of conflict.
    - **Action:** Implement monitoring mechanisms such as performance indicators and regular reports to quickly identify deviations from contract terms.
- **Open Communication**
    - **Objective:** Encourage proactive communication between parties.
    - **Action:** Establish clear and open communication channels where parties can raise concerns without fear of retaliation.

Conflict Resolution Procedures

- **Dispute Resolution Clause**
    - **Objective:** Provide specific methods for resolving disputes in the contract.
    - **Action:** Integrate dispute resolution clauses into the contract, such as mediation, arbitration, or judicial resolution clauses, clearly defining the steps to follow in case of disagreement.
- **Mediation**
    - **Objective:** Resolve conflicts amicably before

engaging in more formal procedures.
- **Action:** Use mediation as a first step, allowing a neutral third party to help the parties find a mutually acceptable agreement.

- **Arbitration**
  - **Objective:** Provide a quick and private alternative to judicial litigation.
  - **Action:** If mediation fails, move to arbitration according to the arbitration clause in the contract. Engage a qualified arbitrator to assess the arguments of both parties and render an enforceable decision.

Documentation and Evidence Collection

- **Document Preservation**
  - **Objective:** Maintain appropriate documentation to support your position in case of a dispute.
  - **Action:** Keep an organized archive of all contract documents, correspondence, performance reports, and evidence of compliance or non-compliance.

- **Conflict Reports**
  - **Objective:** Formally document conflicts and resolution attempts.
  - **Action:** Prepare detailed reports on each conflict, including dates, parties involved, issues raised, actions taken, and outcomes achieved.

Proactive Solutions

- **Conflict Resolution Meetings**
  - **Objective:** Facilitate direct discussions to find solutions.
  - **Action:** Organize specific meetings for conflict

resolution, bringing together all stakeholders to discuss issues and explore solutions.

- **Temporary Agreements**
  - **Objective:** Implement temporary solutions to ease tensions.
  - **Action:** Develop temporary agreements that allow parties to continue working together while discussing long-term solutions. For example, temporarily adjust delivery deadlines or payment terms.

Risk Mitigation

- **Reactive Audits**
  - **Objective:** Identify and correct problems before they become conflicts.
  - **Action:** Implement reactive audits when potential problems are detected to quickly assess the situation and take corrective measures.
- **Conflict Resolution Training**
  - **Objective:** Train teams to identify and resolve conflicts effectively.
  - **Action:** Provide regular training to employees and managers on conflict resolution techniques and negotiation strategies.

Follow-Up and Feedback

- **Post-Resolution Follow-Up**
  - **Objective:** Ensure the implementation and effectiveness of the solutions found.
  - **Action:** After resolving a conflict, closely monitor the implementation of the agreed-upon solutions to ensure they are effective and that issues do not reoccur.
- **Process Evaluation**

- **Objective:** Continuously improve conflict management processes.
- **Action:** Collect feedback from parties involved after resolving a conflict to identify areas for improvement in conflict management processes. Review and adjust procedures based on lessons learned.

Proactive and well-structured dispute and conflict management is crucial to maintaining healthy and effective business relationships. By integrating dispute resolution clauses, encouraging open communication, and establishing clear procedures, you can minimize the negative impacts of conflicts and ensure continuity in contract execution. Prevention, early identification, and effective conflict resolution are key to ensuring the stability and success of long-term contractual relationships.

6.6 Modes of Conflict Resolution

When a conflict arises in the execution of a commercial contract, it is essential to use effective and appropriate conflict resolution methods. These methods can vary depending on the nature of the conflict, the preferences of the parties, and the applicable jurisdiction. Here is an overview of the main conflict resolution methods, along with their advantages and specific considerations:

Negotiation
- **Objective:** Find a mutually acceptable solution by the parties themselves, without external intervention.
- **Method:**
  - **Direct Discussion:** The parties engage in direct and open discussions to resolve the conflict.
  - **Flexibility:** The parties retain full control over the process and the outcomes.
  - **Confidentiality:** Negotiation is generally private, and discussions remain confidential.
- **Advantages:**
  - Speed and reduced cost.
  - Preservation of the business relationship.
  - Creative solutions tailored to the specific needs of the parties.
- **Disadvantages:**
  - Risk of stalemate if the parties cannot reach a compromise.
  - Absence of a neutral third party can lead to a power imbalance.

Mediation
- **Objective:** Facilitate communication between the parties with the help of a neutral mediator to reach an amicable solution.

- **Method:**
    - **Mediator's Intervention:** An independent mediator helps identify points of blockage, facilitates dialogue, and suggests possible solutions.
    - **Voluntary Procedure:** Participation is voluntary, and the parties must consent to the proposed solutions.
- **Advantages:**
    - Neutrality and impartiality of the mediator.
    - Confidential and informal process.
    - Great flexibility and potential preservation of business relationships.
- **Disadvantages:**
    - Non-binding decision unless the parties agree in writing.
    - Effectiveness depends on the good faith of the parties.

Arbitration

- **Objective:** Obtain an enforceable decision from an arbitrator or arbitral tribunal.
- **Method:**
    - **Arbitral Tribunal:** The parties submit their conflict to one or more arbitrators who render a final and binding decision called an arbitral award.
    - **Formalized Procedure:** Although more flexible than state justice, arbitration follows a formal procedure defined by the parties or the rules of the chosen arbitral institution.
- **Advantages:**
    - Rapid decision and generally lower cost than ordinary justice.

- Confidentiality of the process.
- Specialization of the arbitrator in the field of the dispute.
- **Disadvantages:**
  - Potentially high cost of arbitrators' fees.
  - Few opportunities for appeal against the arbitral decision.

Conciliation

- **Objective:** Find an agreement with the help of a conciliator, often integrated within a conflict resolution institution.
- **Method:**
  - **Conciliator's Role:** The conciliator plays an active role in suggesting solutions and helping the parties reach an agreement.
  - **Collaborative Procedure:** Similar to mediation but with a more incisive participation of the conciliator.
- **Advantages:**
  - Fast and often informal process.
  - Intervention of a third party who can propose concrete and realistic solutions.
  - Conciliation agreement often less costly than a trial.
- **Disadvantages:**
  - Non-binding unless an agreement is formalized.
  - Requires the goodwill of the parties to be effective.

Litigation

- **Objective:** Obtain a judicial decision before state courts.
- **Method:**
  - **Legal Procedure:** The parties engage in a trial

before the courts, following a formal procedure dictated by the Code of Civil or Criminal Procedure.
- **Judicial Decision:** The judge renders a binding and enforceable decision.

- **Advantages:**
  - Binding decision and possibility of appeal.
  - Public process often perceived as fair.
- **Disadvantages:**
  - Long duration and high cost of legal proceedings.
  - Possibility of damaging business relationships.
  - Lack of confidentiality.

Considerations for Choosing a Mode

- **Nature of the Conflict:**
  - Technical or specific conflicts may benefit from arbitration expertise, while relational conflicts are often better handled by mediation.
- **Costs and Duration:**
  - Choose a mode based on available financial resources and the need for a quick or extended resolution.
- **Future Relationship:**
  - Consider the impact of the resolution method on the future relationship between the parties. Mediation and conciliation tend to better preserve business relationships.
- **Legal Compliance:**
  - Ensure that the chosen resolution mode is recognized and applicable in the relevant jurisdictions.

By integrating a well-defined conflict management procedure into your contracts and choosing the most appropriate resolution mode for each situation, you can reduce the risks of prolonged disputes and ensure smoother execution of contractual agreements. The key is to remain flexible, pragmatic, and ensure that the chosen resolution mode best serves the interests of all concerned parties.

CONCLUSION

Mastering the art of revising and amending a commercial contract is an invaluable skill in today's business world. Through this book, you have explored the fundamental structures of commercial contracts, the techniques for analyzing and adjusting clauses, and the strategies for conducting effective negotiations that result in balanced agreements.

A good contract review goes beyond merely identifying errors or omissions; it also involves creating clear, precise, and legally sound documents. By combining a deep understanding of legal elements with practical skills in negotiation and management, you are now better equipped to protect your interests and establish long-lasting business relationships.

Whether you are a legal professional, entrepreneur, or contract manager, integrating these insights into your daily practice will help you avoid common pitfalls, strengthen cooperation with your partners, and secure your contractual commitments. Ultimately, the skills you have acquired through this book will contribute to the growth and stability of your business activities.

By approaching each contract with diligence, expertise, and meticulous attention to detail, you can transform every agreement into a successful and mutually beneficial opportunity, thereby ensuring the continued success of your enterprises and collaborations.

www.ingramcontent.com/pod-product-compliance
Lightning Source LLC
Chambersburg PA
CBHW071936210526
45479CB00002B/699